· THE ·
HUNGRY TRAVELER
FRANCE

· THE ·
HUNGRY TRAVELER
FRANCE

· ▦ ·

Sarah Belk King

Andrews McMeel
Publishing
Kansas City

www.andrewsmcmeel.com

ISBN: 0-8362-2727-1
Library of Congress Catalog Card Number: 96-86639

· Contents ·

*With love to my husband, Thomas King,
who adores my vinaigrette.
Also, to my stepsons Wyatt King and
Harrison King, who listen patiently
to my long-winded explanations at the
dinner table about French culture.
I love you guys, more than anything.*

· ■ ·

IN MEMORY OF
*Gregory Usher,
who was director of École de Cuisine
La Varenne in Paris when I was a
student there in 1980.
Gregory was also director of
Le Cordon Bleu cooking school and
the Ritz Escoffier cooking school,
both in Paris. Gregory died of AIDS
in 1994, but his love of French food
inspired me deeply and I will
remember him always.*

• *Acknowledgments* •

MANY THANKS to Barbara Rodriguez for contracting me to do this book, and to Jennifer Worick, managing editor at becker&mayer!, for her good humor and patience when the dog ate my homework. Also, to my friend and colleague, Nancy Barr, who recommended me for this project. A big hug and a huge thank you to Patty Felts for keeping the office running smoothly, and to her oenophile husband, Mark Felts, for proofreading the wine chapter. Also to Peggy Boon for helping me type the manuscript.

· *Foreword* ·

MY LOVE AFFAIR with French food began about twenty years ago when I attended the Sorbonne in Paris. In addition to improving my French, I took it upon myself to learn everything I could about the country's culture. My journals from those days are not filled with descriptions of wild student escapades, but of food and drink. Detailed entries of nearly every meal—what I ate, when I ate it, what it was like, how I could cook it when I returned to the States—make up the bulk of the pages. Every day after classes I had two missions. One was to visit a cultural mecca: a museum, gallery, or church, for example. The other mission—and the one I remember most—was to visit some kind of food establishment every day: a pastry shop, a bread shop, a butcher shop, or a cookware shop. I took copious notes on everything I saw, smelled, and tasted. Another mission—though not one on the daily to-do list—was to have a drink in every bar ever mentioned by Ernest Hemingway. These afternoons at various cafés were spent deliciously alone, journal in one hand, apéritif in the other. I felt oh-so-sophisticated.

I returned to France several years later and attended École de Cuisine La Varenne, the first cooking school in Paris that was really user-friendly for Americans, thanks to British owner/director, Ann Willan. It was a happy time, full of good friends, inspired instructors, and the best butter, cream, and cheese imaginable. I gained ten pounds and a wealth of knowledge and friends for life.

My work has taken me back to France many, many times since graduation from La Varenne. I am always impressed by the French love of food and dining, and I hope that this book can help share that love, so the traveler can enjoy France as much as I do.

INTRODUCTION

· ■ ·

To FULLY experience France, the traveler must indulge in those things the French themselves enjoy: fashion, people watching, and, of course, food and wine. The word "France," in fact, is almost synonymous with good eating, so much so that food and drink are the reasons that France is often selected as a travel destination. While visits to certain other places—say, Alaska or Saudi Arabia—might be stimulating, they may leave the traveler hankering for something delicious to eat. For travelers in France, eating is often the focus, the raison d'être. Yes, France also has art and shopping and castles and battlefields. But the pleasures of the palate appeal to everyone: young and old, rich and not so rich, the experienced traveler as well as the novice. Long after your trip is over, you're likely to recall afternoons spent at the café more clearly than the shoes you bought on the rue de Rivoli. And the pleasure of a deep, dark, intense, slowly simmered *boeuf bourguignonne* will stay in your memory forever. There have been more than a few gourmands who've planned travel itineraries around their reservations at three-star restaurants! And for most other travelers—students and the budget-minded included—mealtime pretty much serves as a means for planning the day. A typical conversation over breakfast might go something like this: "Will it be the Louvre and then lunch? Or shall we have lunch first, then look at the nineteenth-century paintings and then have tea? And what about tonight? How about a cozy dinner at the bistro around the corner? Or would you prefer to have an apéritif at the hotel bar, then go to a brasserie for dinner and a tasting of Alsatian wines? And when are we going to check out that chic new wine bar we read about?" And so on.

And the fascination with food and drink doesn't stop at restaurants. Shopping for food in France is a feast in itself—the sights, the smells, the flurry of activity in the shops and open-air markets are a far cry from the weekly trip to the grocery store back home. At the *fromagerie* (cheese shop), just look at the cheese mongers handle their wares as if they were precious jewels. At the *marché* (open-air market), watch the farmers arrange their tiny carrots just so. Food in France is treated reverently, respectfully. And for good reason: Even the simplest foods—a fresh croissant, an organically grown apple, a wedge of perfectly aged goat's milk cheese—can be as memorable as shopping on the rue du Faubourg Saint-Honoré or seeing the spires of Notre-Dame.

Since the French take their food very seriously,

they demand a lot from the farmers, fishermen, bakers, and cheese makers who provide their country with food. And while it is true that some foods are becoming overprocessed and industrialized, causing quality to suffer, there is still plenty of great-tasting food and drink available to everyone. The word "everyone" is key here since good eating in France crosses all socioeconomic boundaries. The well-to-do may eat different kinds of food than the farmer, but it may not necessarily be better: A perfectly roasted chicken with sautéed potatoes can be as good—or even tastier than—an expensive cut of beef garnished with costly wild mushrooms.

USING THIS BOOK

The Hungry Traveler: France is designed to help the traveler enjoy the country's gastronomic pleasures, in the restaurant, in the market, and in shops. The Menu Primer A to Z will help the traveler decipher menus at every level, from the simplest country café to the best-known restaurants. Beverages A to Z is just what the traveler needs to order everything from a carafe of tap water to a special-occasion champagne and also provides basic cultural information on how to order wine and what *not* to drink with dinner (the answer: coffee!). Comfort Foods can be a real help if you're homesick for mashed potatoes or craving something simple, light, and easy to digest. In addition, this section includes things you might want if you're feeling out of sorts. Regional/Seasonal Specialties provides the traveler with basic information on the geography, climate, and cuisine of the regions of France. Market Buying Tips describes the various food shops and markets, what they sell, and how to shop in them. (Hint: Take your own grocery bag.) Finally, Useful Words Quick Reference Guide includes terms for practical items like napkin, fork, rest room, reservations, and tip. It also includes a list of foods that you might be in the mood for but don't know how to say in French. And if you're allergic to certain foods—nuts, shellfish, eggs, for example—this alphabetical listing allows you to find the word for the offending food quickly and easily and therefore avoid it. This can save you from a case of hives, an upset stomach, or a trip to the emergency room.

BUT WHY AREN'T THEY FAT?

In most French restaurants, portions are likely to be smaller than those in the average American restaurant. If you're very hungry, it's a good idea to do as the French do and partake of several small courses instead of one or two huge ones. Consider the typical American beef dinner: a big, hulking piece of well-marbled prime rib—so massive that it flops over the dinner plate—plus a baked potato with cream *and* butter *and* cheese *and* bacon plus a salad slathered with thick, creamy dressing. Wonder why the French are slender? Watch them eat, and the answer will be clear. Most meals are composed of several courses, portions tend to be small, and, as a rule, the French don't snack as much as we do. Yes, they eat bread at dinner. Yes, they occasionally have cheese or dessert after a meal. But if your steak weighs in at six ounces instead of sixteen, a little treat after dinner won't throw your diet to the dogs.

Dining in France need not be fattening or unhealthy or expensive or confusing. With this guide in hand, you can make choices that suit your palate, your appetite, and your pocketbook.

BREAKFAST, LUNCH, AND DINNER

When breakfast—*petit déjeuner* (peh-TEE DAY-jhuh-NAY)— is included in the price of your hotel room, it will usually be a continental breakfast, or *petit déjeuner continental* (peh-TEE DAY-jhuh-NAY KON-tee-nihn-TAHL). This generally is a simple affair consisting of coffee, tea, or hot chocolate plus a croissant, roll, or other bread. It may be simple, but oh, how delicious simplicity can be! Your coffee will not be poured from a pot that's been sitting on the burner all morning long, and your bread will not be full of additives and preservatives. Your coffee will be made fresh, to order; milk for your coffee will be steamed just so. If you're a tea drinker, your tea will be served in a proper pot with fresh lemon wedges or milk (no imitation-dairy whiteners here), and should you opt for hot chocolate, it just might be made with melted chocolate bars. As for breakfast breads, croissants made in France today are still better than those found anywhere else in the world, although if you listen carefully, you may hear old-timers complain that the croissants today aren't as flaky, buttery, or as fresh as they used to be. Never mind; they're still delicious. They need no embellishment, but you can slather them with butter, jam, or honey if you want to. But croissants are only one part of a typical continental breakfast. Other offerings might include rolls, *minibrioche*, *pain au chocolat*, and little packaged toasts that you might want to tuck into your backpack. They'll come in handy later on if your blood sugar drops as you gaze at the Winged Victory, the Arc de Triomphe, or Jim Morrison's grave. More substantial continental breakfasts may include juice (orange, grapefruit, and tomato are the most common), yogurt, and fresh fruit. Most hotels offer other breakfast foods if you simply must have your eggs, oatmeal, or corn flakes.

Lunch—*déjeuner* (DAY-jhuh-NAY)—in France usually begins about 12:30, although some restaurants may begin serving at noon. Most office workers break for lunch at 12:30 or 1:00, so to get a table at a popular restaurant, café, or bistro without reservations, it is recommended that you get there by noon. Many kitchens close promptly at 2:00 P.M., so if you're tied up at the Louvre until three, you may need to have lunch at a café or brasserie, most of which serve all day long. How hungry you are may also determine where you eat. Cafés are a good choice if you just want a sandwich or a salad. (Fullfledged restaurants won't be very happy if you order something minimal since they'd rather fill their tables with diners having a three-course meal.)

In a hurry? Lunch can often be had at the farmers' market or from street vendors. Savory crêpes, slices of *pissaladière* (French-style pizza), and sandwiches made with spit-cooked meats are just a few of the selections you might find as you wander the streets. And if you're at the market, a bit of cheese, a hunk of bread, and some fresh fruit can be a delicious feast. For a real sit-down lunch, expect to dine for about two hours. Some restaurants offer a *dégustation*, or tasting menu, at lunchtime, so if eating is the activity for the day, you can order five, six, or up to eight courses and keep sipping espresso, wine, or brandy until the restaurant sets up for dinner!

Dinner—*Dîner* (DEE-nay)—in France usually begins at 8:30, but most establishments will accept reservations for as early as 7:30. (Dining hours may be earlier outside the big cities.) If you're going to the theater or you simply want to eat late, have the concierge check the hours of the restaurant where you want to dine. Some kitchens close at 10:00; in small towns, even earlier. Your best bet for a late meal is to go to a café or brasserie, which generally serve food until 11:00 P.M. or later. And then there's always room service. Most hotels offer something late at night, such as smoked salmon, simple sandwiches, and sometimes caviar. If you are the type of traveler who likes to eat on a regular schedule, plan ahead. It's easy to have the concierge take care of reservations for you. Or, make them yourself as you stroll about during the day. Nothing is worse than being very hungry and very tired and discovering that all the restaurants are either full or closed, in which case your dinner will be peanuts and screw-top wine from the minibar.

COCKTAILS AND DRINKS

Cocktail time exists in France, and although you won't see signs for "happy hour" as such, cafés and bars do tend to fill up in late afternoon and early evening after work. While the American-style cocktail is not a traditional preprandial drink in France, some of the simpler American concoctions—like highballs—are available. The most popular drinks taken before dinner, however, are those known as "apéritifs." The French are likely to have a kir, a vermouth on the rocks with a twist, or a Pernod. Apéritifs tend to be light and lower in alcohol than true cocktails, and they won't numb your palate like harsh spirits or spoil your appetite like some sticky-sweet, high-calorie American cocktails. For more on apéritifs, see Beverages A to Z.

EATING ESTABLISHMENTS

Just as an American coffee shop differs from a cafe-teria, which differs from a restaurant, in France there are various levels of dining from the simple café to the grand restaurant. While there is some crossover (some big-city cafés serve full-fledged, multicourse meals, and some country restaurants serve very simple fare), generally speaking, there are certain differences between café, bistro, brasserie, *salon de thé,* and restaurant. For example, a small café in Dijon will have a menu similar to that of a small café in Lyons; a bistro in Brittany will offer fare similar to that of a bistro in Normandy, and so forth. A description of the various eating establishments follows, starting with the simplest type of eatery and working up to the most formal.

Café (kah-FAY). The word *café* means coffee, which is sold throughout the day in many forms. The word also refers to the establishment itself. The café is certainly where one can always—at any time of day—get a jolt of caffeine. But the café is much more than just a place to get a caffeine fix; it's a place for chatting about sports, horse racing, politics, boyfriends, and the latest fashions. The café is where one meets a friend before going out to dinner or to the movies. The café is where the solitary traveler can grab a table and write postcards for hours while sipping a single *café au lait.* The café is where one can go when it starts to rain and there's no umbrella in your briefcase or backpack. The café often has tables and chairs out-of-doors, where the locals like to take their potables all year long except in the harshest weather. (It's not uncommon to see Parisians wrapped in coats, hats, and scarves in the dead of winter sipping hot tea or an apéritif as they watch the scene on the street. (Outdoors may be the only place nonsmokers won't be surrounded by cigarette smoke, as cafés don't usually have non-smoking sections.)

Cafés range from the very basic to the very chic. At their simplest, cafés are neighborhood hangouts where locals knock back an espresso or a glass of wine or whiskey and talk about everything from soccer to the weather to life in general. Fancy big-city cafés are expensive (an espresso might cost the equivalent of four dollars or so), so the clientele is typically the see-and-be-seen crowd, the ladies who lunch, white-collar workers on expense accounts, tourists with deep pockets, or anyone who simply wants to rub shoulders with the beautiful people. Most waiters and waitresses in big-city cafés speak some English, and many will offer a menu in English.

As for the menu, cafés offer coffee, tea, hot chocolate, soft drinks, mineral water, fruit juices, apéritifs, wine, and spirits. As for food, in the morning you can expect some kind of breakfast bread, and maybe a few egg dishes if the café is sizable. At midday, the menu gets a little bigger. Simple cafés will offer a few types of sandwiches, while the chic cafés in Paris will have sandwiches plus things like smoked salmon, several kinds of salad, soups, and some simple dishes like grilled chicken with fries. In the afternoon, the café is the perfect place to relax with a hot or cold drink, alcoholic or nonalcoholic. Dinner is not usually served in small cafés, but the larger ones often have a separate dining area for real eating.

Spending time at a French café is essential to having a true French experience. The idea is not so much what you eat or drink as much as getting together with friends, people watching, relaxing, or simply killing time in one of the most delightful ways possible.

Bistro (BEE-stroh). Generally speaking, a bistro is a smallish restaurant that serves casual food. Many bistros are family-owned and have a regular clientele. But just because they're casual doesn't mean they're lacking in style. Just as cafés range from very basic to chic, bistros vary, too, according to where they're located and their reputation for good food and good times. All bistros, however, tend to have simple interiors; even the fanciest bistros in Paris cover their tables with sheets of white paper rather than tablecloths and set them with rustic tableware. The menu at a bistro is likely to include things like country pâté, rustic salads with warm bacon dressing, onion soup, steak with fries, chocolate mousse, and simple fruit tarts. House wines are served by the carafe or the glass and are usually very good. Bistros are a good choice for quick, casual meals that won't cost an arm and a leg.

Brasserie (BRAH-suh-REE). Brasseries are similar to bistros in that they're relatively casual eateries. The word "brasserie" means "brewery," and most brasseries have some kind of link with Alsace in northeastern France (near Germany) and beer making. Brasseries also serve a variety of Alsatian wines such as Gewürztztraminer and Riesling. Brasserie fare tends to be substantial, and the menu will probably include at least one Alsatian dish such as *choucroute garnie* or *coq au Riesling*. Brasseries may also offer specialties of the region in which they are located as well as many traditional French favorites, like raw oysters. Brasseries are usually open late (around one or two A.M.), so they're a good choice for grabbing a bite after the movies. Just don't expect a brasserie to be quiet or calm; they're lively, brassy, noisy, crowded establishments where people come to eat, drink, and have fun. Most likely, the traveler will have fun there, too.

Restaurants (REHS-tah-RAHN). The word "restaurant" is used to describe an eating establishment that is *not* a bistro or a brasserie or a café. Sound confusing? It's not, really. Generally speaking, very fancy eating places are restaurants. Also in the restaurant category are those places serving modern or innovative fare (sometimes called "nouvelle cuisine") that doesn't fit into the steak-and-fries bistro niche or the sausage-and-sauerkraut brasserie category. An establishment that specializes in fish and seafood or in ethnic fare such as Moroccan or Vietnamese will also be called a "restaurant."

Bistro à vin (BEE-stroh ah-VAN). Wine bar. This hangout is more than just a bar that serves wine. Wine bars often have full-fledged menus, and in Paris and other big cities, wine bars are often chic, happening places serving a well-heeled clientele. Wine bars are similar to the neighborhood café, except that instead of one or two wines by the glass, many will be offered. And what to eat at a wine bar?

Usually charcuterie fare: cheeses, salads, stews, and other simple fare.

Salon de thé (sah-LOHN deh TAY). Tea salon or tearoom. The French tearoom is not just a place for old ladies and mothers with well-behaved children. Tea drinking is as stylish as it was a hundred years ago, and many urban tearooms—especially in Paris—serve power lunches to white-collar business types before setting the table for afternoon tea.

Tea is, of course, a specialty at a tearoom, and the traveler will be able to choose from many types, with caffeine and without. Tearooms also serve coffee and hot chocolate and little sandwiches, pastries, and cookies. And don't forget, most tearooms sell loose tea in pretty tins, which make terrific gifts to take back home.

A Word About Making Reservations

If you want to dine at a very famous restaurant, reservations must be made in advance (sometimes up to three months ahead) in writing, specifying the date, time, and number in your party. For other restaurants, call—or have the concierge at your hotel call—a few days ahead of time. If your dinner plans change, call the restaurant, brasserie, or bistro and cancel your reservation.

MENUS AND ORDERING

Which kind of menu you choose depends on how hungry you are, how much money you want to spend, and how curious you are about trying lots of different foods. Depending on the size and location of the eating establishment, the kinds of menus are as follows:

À la carte (ah lah KAHRT). Just as in the States, ordering à la carte means that each item on the menu is priced separately. This is a good way to order if there are specific things on the menu that you do and do not like, if you have any food allergies, or if you simply aren't very hungry and want a salad and a main course and that's it.

Dégustation (DAY-goo-STAH-see-ohn). Called a "tasting menu" in the U.S.A., this kind of menu features many small courses that allow the diner to taste lots of different things, many of which will likely be specialties of the house. There are usually at least five courses in a tasting menu, and there may be as many as eight to ten. If you choose the *menu dégustation*, be prepared to spend several hours at the table, and do not expect the menu to be "balanced." For example, you may be served three shellfish courses, three game courses, and three desserts. Where's the roughage? Where are the veggies? While tasting menus can be fun, the point is to try things, not to have a balanced meal. There may be few or no vegetables other than a baby carrot here and a sprig of fresh cilantro there. Not to worry. You can have a salad and mineral water for lunch the next day. However, this is not to say that all tasting menus are fattening or unhealthy; many French chefs are trim, slim marathoners who are as concerned about your digestion as they are their own.

Plat du jour (plah doo JHOOR). This is the "special of the day," which is often listed on a chalkboard in casual bistros and brasseries. In more formal restaurants, the daily special will be printed on the menu or rattled off verbally by the waiter.

Prix fixe (PREE feeks). This phrase means "fixed price" and refers to a complete meal served for a preset price. A prix fixe menu is nearly always three courses and sometimes four or five, which would include a first course, main course, and dessert, plus perhaps a starter (such as oysters or a bit of caviar), a fish course, and/or a cheese course. The prix fixe menu is indeed something to consider if you like what's being offered and you're relatively hungry.

Spécialités de la maison (SPEH-see-AH-lee-TAY deh lah may-SOHN). Specialties of the house. These are dishes that the restaurant claims to prepare particularly well or those that have earned the chef some kind of reputation as a good cook. A *spécialité* might also refer to a dish that a very cherished old restaurant has been serving for many years and for which it is famous.

Table d'hôte (tah-bul DOHT). This term literally means "the host's table" and refers to a meal consisting of several courses for the price of the main course.

DINING-OUT NOTES
Bread and Butter

Bread, no matter how simple, will be offered at every meal. In fancy restaurants, you'll be served rolls on a bread-and-butter plate instead of a basket of bread plopped down to be shared by all the diners at the table. And while bread is a must in France, butter for your bread isn't always offered. If you want butter and don't see it on the table, just say the word *beurre* (burr) to the waiter. Very small establishments still charge a nominal fee for butter, and be aware that in most of France the butter will be unsalted. If you aren't accustomed to its natural sweetness, simply sprinkle your buttered bread with a bit of salt.

Drinks at the Table

It's perfectly fine to sip an apéritif at the table while you peruse the menu or wait for other guests to join you. After one or two apéritifs, the French usually order wine and/or mineral water to accompany the meal. Certainly, it is acceptable to abstain from anything alcoholic. Instead of (or in addition to) mineral water, teetotalers can opt for fruit juice or a soft drink. Iced tea is not as widely available in France; have something else instead. Whatever you do, do not order coffee before or with lunch or dinner—it is always drunk after the meal.

Smoking

Although they smoke less than they did a decade ago, the French smoke more than Americans, and they seem more cavalier about lighting up and blowing smoke in your direction. They consider smoking to be their right, and most nonsmoking French are accustomed to it and don't complain much. I personally loathe cigarette, cigar, and pipe smoke and find it ruins my palate, burns my eyes, and makes my head ache. I always ask for a table in the nonsmoking area (if there is one), the tables designated for *non-fumeurs*, or nonsmokers. Small cafés and country restaurants are not likely to have a nonsmoking area, so be prepared. In good weather, nonsmokers should look for a table outside, where the smoke can at least circulate better. In any case, except in tiptop, expensive restaurants, complaints about your neighbors' smoke will probably fall on deaf ears. Try to be patient, and if the waiter won't seat you at another table, eat quickly, pay your bill, be nice, tip the waiter (it's not his fault that there are smokers in your face), and have dessert and coffee somewhere less smoky.

Salad

The French often have a simple green salad after the main course, before (or sometimes with) the cheese course. There are some salads that might be offered to start a meal, but these will usually be composed salads of some sort, perhaps with duck, foie gras, walnuts, marinated vegetables, or quail eggs, not a simple green salad. These first-course French "salads" focus more on the added ingredients than the salad greens. Do try the French tradition of having salad before dessert; it is a delicious way to cleanse the palate after a rich or complicated main course, and it eases the diner gracefully to cheese or dessert. Do note that these palate-cleansing salads are tossed with oil and vinegar dressings; do not even *think* of asking for blue cheese dressing or ranch or Green Goddess or Thousand Island, as such a request will be met with frowns and general negativity.

Paying and Tipping

Most restaurants—but not all—accept credit cards. If you have questions, ask before you are seated. Try to familiarize yourself with the exchange rate before going to a restaurant so that if you're paying in cash, you won't be confused. A menu that says *service compris* means that the service charge, or tip, has already been added to the price printed (on the menu) for each dish. The term *service non compris* means that the tip will be added on at the end, after the food and beverages have been totaled. Whichever way the restaurant operates, you will be paying the 12 to 15 percent built-in tip. If the service has been particularly good, or if the restaurant is a noted one, it is certainly nice to leave up to 5 percent of the bill as an extra tip. Likewise, if the maître d' or wine steward has been especially helpful, an extra bit of cash—twenty francs in the palm as you shake hands good-bye—is a kind gesture. You are not, however, expected to leave anything extra.

Dressing Up, Dressing Down

It may seem somewhat surprising that in a country where dining is so important, dress codes for dinner are a bit more casual than in the U.S.A. Even three-star restaurants tend toward the casual; some do not require a jacket and tie (although men might feel more at ease in both). And while jeans are not appropriate in these temples of gastronomy, a "smart casual" look (such as khaki slacks and a nicely cut jacket for men) is certainly acceptable. Ladies can wear slacks just about anywhere, but it is important to keep in mind that the French are very fashion conscious, and while dressing formally may not be necessary, ladies will probably feel more at ease when dressed stylishly, with appropriate accessories. Obviously, in casual cafés, bistros, brasseries and wine bars, jeans and a nicely cut shirt, sweater, or jacket are fine. Remember that except for students, the French usually only wear sneakers in the gym or on the courts. As for shorts and sandals, they're fine if you're young and gorgeous and have perfect legs and you're at the beach. In town—and especially in big cities—shorts are acceptable if they're longish and nicely cut of good fabric. Sandals should be somewhat sophisticated (i.e., no thongs) and should provide some kind of protection from the dog poop in the streets and on the sidewalks.

Dogs

Speaking of dogs, they are allowed in most French restaurants, so don't be surprised if you see Fifi on Madame's lap in a venerable old brasserie.

Rest Rooms

The term for toilet is "W.C.," from the British "water closet." The French pronounce it "Vay Say," as the letters W and C are pronounced in French. If you need to go, look at the waiter and say "Vay Say?" with a questioning look on your face. You will be given an answer in English or manual directions with the pointing of a finger. Frequently, even in well-respected establishments, rest rooms are unisex; that is, they are shared by both men and women. But don't panic; they are usually one-stall affairs with a door that locks, so you will have privacy. Sometimes, however, even when the actual toilets for men and women are separate, there will be only one sink—to be shared by both sexes—for hand washing.

MENU PRIMER A TO Z
(FRENCH TO ENGLISH)
· ▪ ·

LOOKING AT a menu in a foreign country can be daunting, particularly if you don't know the language. And even if you *have* studied the language, when you're hungry and tired it's easy to get frazzled as you try to remember your adjectives and adverbs.

The Menu Primer—translator—that follows is designed to help the traveler order a meal and shop for food. The words for the most common foods, cooking techniques, and regional preparations are all included here, as are words you might see on a menu, like *service compris* (service included) or *prix fixe* (fixed-price menu). Once you've decided what to eat, you'll probably want to order a bottle of wine or other potable to accompany your meal. For detailed descriptions of the various drinks offered in France, turn to Beverages A to Z.

You've probably heard that the French are rude, that they hate Americans, and that they think they're better and know more than everyone. Wrong, wrong, wrong. Such generalizations are like saying all Texans are cowboys, all Californians are airheads, all New Yorkers talk fast, and all Southerners are slow and stupid. Don't spoil your trip with preconceived ideas of what and who the French are. Anyone—whether French, American, British, or South African—can be cranky and short-tempered or gentle and kind. If you find yourself in the presence of someone having a bad day, spread your good cheer, and it will more than likely rub off. When a waiter, wine steward, or vendor seems impatient, don't be put off; instead, try to remember that they're just trying to do their job and get orders in quickly and efficiently. I've discovered that even the snootiest waiters and *sommeliers* ease up if I insist on being polite and cheerful. If you spread your goodwill, others will generally follow suit. Consider this: The average waiter encounters many, many insistent people during the day who make demands that can't be met, such as requests for such non-French items as Green Goddess salad dressing, diet Dr. Pepper, and American coffee. Instead of frustrating yourself and the waiter, why not exercise patience and try to eat the way the locals eat? You'll inevitably encounter some new foods, and you'll probably have more fun, too.

· Pronunciation Guide ·

Vowels

French Spelling	Phonetic Symbol	Sound Description
a, â	ah	like a in almond
e, eu, oeu	uh	like a in about or e in the
è, ê	e	like e in pet
é, er	ay	like a in make
i, y	ee	like ee in peep
o	o	like o in more
o, au, eau	oh	like o in low
oi	wa	like wa in want
ou	oo	like oo in moon
u	oo	no English equivalent; pronounce ee, then oh

Consonants

ç	s	like s
ch	sh	like sh in shame
gn	ny	like the n sound in onion
gu	g	like g in gone
j	jh	like the sio sound in television
qu	k	like k in ketchup
s	s or z	like English s unless between two vowels, when it is pronounced like z, as in magazine

Note: In most cases, only the singular form of verbs is provided in this book unless the singular and plural forms vary greatly in pronounciation. Likewise, the feminine form of adjectives has not, as a rule, been given.

Agneau (ahn-YOH). Lamb. The French have excellent lamb. Try it medium rare (*à point*) if you've never had it that way. When lamb chops are rosy and pink, the texture is juicier and the flavor tends to be more pronounced.

Aigre (AG-ruh). Sour.

Ail (i-EE). Garlic. The traveler will encounter lots of dishes made with garlic in southern France, where it is consumed with great passion. Just remember, "garlic breath" isn't as noticeable if everyone eats garlic, so pass the garlic around the table.

Aillade (i-ee-YAHD). A sauce made of garlic, walnuts, and walnut oil that is sometimes served with duck. (See Regional/Seasonal Specialties: The Southwest.)

Aïoli (i-oh-LEE). Mayonnaise flavored with garlic, usually served alongside salt cod and hard-boiled eggs. In Provence, this is a much-loved sauce. If you love garlic and want to make this when you get home, it's easy to do in the food processor. (See Regional/Seasonal Specialties: Languedoc and Provence.)

Alcool (ahl-KOHL). Alcohol. The word *alcool* is not generally used to order drinks at a bar. Instead, ask for the spirit by name, such as "un whisky" or "un vodka."

Aligot (ah-lee-GOHT). A specialty of the Auvergne made with mashed potatoes and a cheese of the same name, *aligot*. This cheese and potato dish is hearty and filling and a good choice if you've been skiing or hiking all day in the mountains. (See Regional/Seasonal Specialties: Central France.)

Allumette (al-yoo-METT). Literally, "match," used to describe fried potatoes cut into matchstick shapes. Also, strips of puff pastry.

(à la) Alsacienne (ah la al-zah-SYEHN). In the Alsacienne style. Dishes made with sauerkraut, sausage, and sometimes Riesling wine. (See Regional/Seasonal Specialties: Alsace-Lorraine.)

Amande (ah-MAHN). Almond. The French use almonds in pastry making more so than any other nut. Many Gallic desserts are made with almonds or almond-flavored buttercream.

Amer (ah-MEHR). Bitter; a term often used to describe unsweetened chocolate.

(à l') Américaine (AH-meh-ree-KEHN). A rich sauce of white wine, cognac, tomatoes, and butter often served with lobster.

Amuse-gueule (AH-mooz-GUHL). Little appetizers or snacks, often served with apéritifs. The term actually means "amuse the mouth," and that's exactly what these little morsels do.

Ananas (ah-nah-NAH). Pineapple. This tropical fruit is used in dessert making and may be offered fresh with other fruits as a dessert. Remember, fresh pineapple is said to aid digestion, so if you've over-indulged, try a slice or two of fresh pineapple for dessert instead of the chocolate mousse.

Anchoïde or *anchoyade* (ahn-SHWAD or ahn-sho-YAHD). A mixture of oil, anchovies, and garlic often served with raw vegetables or spread on toast. A specialty of Provence.

(à l') ancienne (ahn-see-EHN). In the "old style" or "old school." The term is often used to describe braised beef and fricassees.

Andouillette (ahn-dwee-YETT). Sausages made from pork and pork intestines. These sausages are usually served grilled and accompanied by strong mustard. If you like chitterlings, you may like *andouillettes*. If you don't like chitterlings, there will never be enough strong mustard on your *andouillette* to hide the taste.

Aneth (ah-NETH). The herb dill.

(à l') Anglaise (ahn-GLEHZ). Literally, "in the English style." The term refers to food prepared with

little embellishment. It can also refer to foods—often fish—dipped in bread crumbs and fried. Although the French may poke a little fun at the plainness of English cooking, foods cooked *à l'anglaise* can be absolutely delicious. Crème anglaise is a light, sweet custard sauce.

Anna (ah-NAH). A term used to describe a potato dish (*pommes Anna*) in which potatoes are cut into thin rounds then layered with butter. The dish is baked and then inverted for serving. It is often served with roasts.

Apéritif (ah-PAY-ruh-teef). A drink served before a meal that is said to stimulate the appetite; e.g., vermouth, Dubonnet, Campari, and anisette (*anis*). (See also Beverages A to Z.)

À point (ah PWAHN). Medium rare. The French tend to eat their meat a tad on the rare side, so be advised that chops, steaks, or fish cooked medium rare in France might be pinker than you would have in a restaurant in the States. *À point* can also refer to cheese or fruit that is perfectly ripe, at a good stage for eating.

(à l') arlésienne (ahrl-see-EHN). In the style of Arles. The term is usually used to describe dishes prepared with tomatoes, onions, eggplant, potatoes, rice, and sometimes olives. (See Regional/Seasonal Specialties: Provence.)

Artichaut (AR-tee-SHOW). Artichoke. The French work wonders with artichokes, and they are likely to appear on menus all over France. Since most of the edible part is on the artichoke bottom, you'll usually see the term *fond d'artichaut* (fond DAR-tee-SHOW) on the menu, which means "artichoke bottoms."

Artichauts à la barigoule (AR-tee-SHOW ah lah BAH-ree-GOOL). Artichokes stuffed with mushrooms, ham, onions, and garlic, then cooked in oil and water. (See Regional/Seasonal Specialties: Provence.)

Asperge (ah-SPAIRJH). Asparagus. You'll see both white and green asparagus in France, particularly in the spring. White asparagus is expensive since it has to be grown entirely underground and the growing process is quite labor-intensive.

Assaisonnement (ah-SAY-sohn-MAHN). Condiment, seasoning.

Assiette (AH-see-YETT). Plate, dish. As in English, this word can refer to an offering of food, such as "a plate of ham," or an actual piece of tableware, as in "I need a plate."

Assorti(e) (AH-sor-TEE). Assorted, mixed.

Aubergine (OH-bair-JHEEN). Eggplant. Cooks in southern France are particularly fond of eggplant, and you're likely to encounter lots of it in Provence, stuffed, baked, stewed—any way you can imagine.

Aurore (oh-ROAR). Literally, "dawn," sauce made with tomatoes and cream. It is sometimes served as a sauce for hard-boiled eggs and served as a first course. Leave it to the French to turn a humble hard-boiled egg into something special.

(à l') Auvergnate (OH-vair-NYAH). In the style of the Auvergne. Such dishes are often made with cabbage and sausage. (See Regional/Seasonal Specialties: Central France.)

Avocat (ah-voh-KAH). Avocado. Often served as a garnish or in salads.

Babas au rhum (bah-bah zoh rum). Buttery, rum-soaked yeast cakes.

Baeckeoff (bay-KOFF). Literally, "baker's oven," a stew of beef, lamb (or mutton), and pork, potatoes, and onions, originally cooked in a baker's oven. (See Regional/Seasonal Specialties: Alsace-Lorraine.)

Bagna cauda (BAHN-yah KOW-dah). This Italian dish is also a specialty of southern France. It is a warm dipping sauce made of anchovies, olive oil, and garlic served with raw vegetables.

Baguette (ba-GETT). Literally, "stick" or "wand." The term refers to a long, thin loaf of white bread with a crackly crust and rather chewy interior. This is the classic French loaf, and the French eat lots of it. Taste it, and you'll see why.

Baie (bay). Berry.

Baigné (BAN-yay). Bathed. A term used to describe a dish—usually fish—that is cooked or served in a liquid, as if it were "bathed."

Ballottine (bah-loh-TEEN). A kind of loaf of meat, fish, game, or poultry that is braised or roasted. It is usually served hot but can be served cold as well.

Banane (bah-NAHN). Banana. You'll find fresh bananas at the market and in some desserts.

Banon (ba-NOH). A small, round goat's milk cheese (or cheese made with a mixture of goat's and cow's milk) wrapped in chestnut leaves. It is named after the village of Puimichel near Banon in Provence. (See also Market Buying Tips: *Fromageries*.)

Barbue (bar-boo). Brill, a flatfish in the same family as turbot.

Barquette (bahr-KEHT). Small, boat-shaped pastry shells filled with either sweet or savory fillings. (The word *barquette* literally means "little boat.")

Basilic (bah-see-LEEK). Basil. This herb is used a great deal in Provence, where basil is prolific and the Italian influence on food is very prominent.

(À la) Basquaise (ah lah bah-SKASE). In the Basque style, with tomatoes, ham, and rice. (See Regional/Seasonal Specialties: The Pays Basque, Gascony, and the Pyrénées.)

Bavaroise (BAH-vah-wah). Bavarian. A rich, cold, molded custard dessert often served with fruit or a fruit sauce.

Bavette (bah-VETT). Skirt steak. An expensive, lean cut of beef that might be served in casual bistros.

Béarnaise (bair-NAYZ). A thick sauce made of egg yolks, shallots, white wine, butter, tarragon, and vinegar. It is usually served with steak and, sometimes, lamb.

Bécasse (beh-KAHS). Woodcock, a small game bird.

Béchamel (BAY-shah-MEHL). A thick white sauce made with flour, butter, and milk and usually flavored with bay leaves and nutmeg. This classic sauce is the foundation for many traditional French dishes.

Beignet (ben-YAY). A sweet or savory fritter.

Belon (beh-LOHN). Oysters from the river in Brittany of the same name. (See also Regional/Seasonal Specialties: Brittany).

Bercy (bair-SEE). A sauce made of fish stock, white wine, shallots, and seasonings, often served with fish or seafood.

Betterave (bett-RAHV). Beet. Cooked beets are often julienned or diced and tossed with a vinaigrette dressing and eaten as a room-temperature salad. They are sometimes available in this form in charcuteries.

Beurre (burr). Butter. Most butter used in France—both in cooking and on the table—is unsalted. Salted butter is called *beurre demi-sel* (BURR dehmee-sell), or slightly salted. Butter is a specialty of Charente. (See Regional/Seasonal Specialties: The Southwest.)

Beurre blanc (BURR blahn). A rich sauce traditionally made with butter, shallots, and vinegar, often served with fish, vegetables, eggs, and poultry.

Beurre noir (BURR nwahr). Browned butter sauce, lemon juice (or vinegar), parsley, and sometimes capers. It is sometimes served with skate, or *raie*.

Bien cuit (byehn KWEE). Cooked well done, as in steak or lamb.

Bifteck (BEEF-tek). Steak, usually of beef. Even though the steak from Charolais cattle (in Burgundy) is said to be the finest in France, most steak aficionadoes still think American beef is the best in the world.

Biologique (BEE-oh-lah-JHEEK). Organic. The traveler can find organically grown foods in specialty foods stores and health foods stores throughout France.

Biscuit (bee-SKWEE). This term can mean a cookie, a cracker, or a type of sponge cake.

Biscuit à la cuillère (bee-SKWEE ah lah koo-YAIR). Lady finger. These delicate little finger-shaped cakes are often used to make desserts such as charlottes.

Biscuit de Savoie (bee-SKWEE deh Sah vwoy) A light sponge cake. (See Regional/Seasonal Specialties: Franche-Comté, Savoy, and the Dauphine.)

Blanc de volaille (BLAHN deh vo-LI-yee). Chicken breast.

Blanquette (blahn-KETT). A stew of veal, lamb, chicken, or seafood, served in a sauce made with cream and egg yolks.

Blé (blay). Wheat.

Blette (blehtt). Swiss chard. This leafy vegetable is often served in southern France mixed with apples, pine nuts, cheese, and raisins in a deep, double-crust pie that—depending on the amount of sugar added—can be either an appetizer or dessert.

Bleu (bluh). A term used to describe steak (or sometimes lamb) cooked rare. Note: Meats cooked *bleu* will be nearly raw on the inside. If what you want is rare, use the word *saignant* (say-NYAHN).

Blinis (BLEE-nee). Small, rather thick pancakes usually made with buckwheat flour and served with caviar.

Boeuf (buhf). Beef.

Boeuf à la ficelle (BUHF ah lah fee-SELL). Beef tied with string and poached. This is an old-fashioned dish that is simple, clean, and delicious. It's quite welcome if you've had a lot of rich, complicated foods.

Boeuf à la flamande (BUHF ah lah flah-MAHND). Beef braised with beer and vegetables. (See Regional/ Seasonal Specialties: Champagne, the North, the Île de France.)

Boeuf à la mode (BUHF ah lah mode). Beef braised in red wine, then served with carrots, onions, turnips, and mushrooms. An old-fashioned dish that tastes as if it was made by someone's grandmother.

Boisson (bwah-SOHN). Drink.

Bonbon (BON-bon). Candy.

Bonite (boh-NEET) *or Bonita* (boh-NEE-tah). Bonito, a kind of fish similar to tuna.

Bonne femme (bohn FEHM). Literally, "good woman." A term used to describe the simple, hearty flavors of home cooking. It can refer to a garnish of bacon, potatoes, mushrooms, and onions served with meat. It can also refer to a mixture of shallots, parsley, mushrooms, and potatoes served with fish. *Sauce bonne femme* is a sauce made with white wine, shallots, mushrooms, and lemon juice.

(à la) Bordelaise (ah lah bohr-dah-LAYZ). In the style of Bordeaux, dishes prepared or served with a brown sauce of red or white wine, shallots, and bone marrow. (See also Regional/Seasonal Specialties: The Southwest.)

Bouchée (boo-SHAY). Something that is bite-sized, such as hors d'oeuvres or pastries.

Boudin blanc (boo-DAHN blahn). A delicate sausage made from pork, chicken, veal, or game.

Boudin noir (boo-DAHN nwahr). Sausage made with pork and pork blood, usually served grilled. This sausage has a very earthy flavor, similar to black pudding, and is not recommended for those who don't enjoy strong, meaty tastes.

Bouillabaisse (BOO-lyuh-BAYZ). A classic French fish soup that can be prepared with many different combinations of fish and shellfish. It is a specialty of southern France and is traditionally infused with garlic, tomatoes, olive oil, and saffron. (See also Regional/Seasonal Specialties: Provence.)

Bouillon (BOO-yohn). Strained broth made with meat, poultry, fish, or vegetables. Ask for this clear soup if you're not feeling well or if you're watching your fat intake.

(à la) Boulangère (ah lah boo-lahn-JHAIR). Literally, "in the style of the baker's wife." The term usually refers to meat or poultry baked or braised with potatoes and onions. Such dishes were originally baked in the baker's bread oven, then brought home to eat.

(à la) Bourgeoise (ah lah boor-JHWAZ). Literally "in the style of the middle class," referring to good, basic, home-style cooking, usually with carrots, onions, and bacon.

(à la) Bourguignonne (ah lah boor-gee-NYON). In the Burgundy style, usually with red wine, mushrooms, bacon, and small onions, e.g., *boeuf bourguignon*. (See also Regional/Seasonal Specialties: Burgundy and the Lyonnais.)

Bourride (BOO-reed). A fish soup that can include a variety of fish. *Bourride* is a specialty of southern France and is usually flavored with tomatoes, garlic, olive oil, and onions. It is often served with aïoli sauce.

Braisé (brah-ZAY). Braised.

Brandade de morue (brahn-DAHD deh mo-ROO). A specialty of the Languedoc region, which combines a puree of salt cod and garlic, plus cream and/or oil. Mashed potatoes or truffles are sometimes added.

(à la) Bretonne (ah lah bray-TON). Dishes prepared in the style of Brittany. This usually refers to a sauce of white wine, carrots, leeks, and celery or to a dish served with white beans. (See also Regional/Seasonal Specialties: Brittany).

Brie (bree). A large disk of buttery-soft cheese with a downy white rind and pale yellow interior. (See Regional/Seasonal Specialties: Champagne and Market Buying Tips: *Fromageries*.)

Brioche (BREE-ohsh). A yeast bread enriched with butter and eggs. Brioche is made into large loaves as well as smaller, roll-sized buns. Some continental breakfast offerings include a small brioche.

(à la) Broche (ah lah BROSH). Cooked on a spit, such as a baby lamb, pig, or chicken.

Brochette (broh-SHEHT). Meats or vegetables cooked on a skewer.

Brocoli (broh-koh-LEE). Broccoli. This vegetable is sometimes served as a side dish.

Brouillé (broo-YAY). Scrambled. This term is most often used on menus to describe scrambled eggs. (See Comfort Foods: Egg.)

Brûlé (broo-LAY). Literally, "burned." The term usually refers to desserts that have been placed under a hot fire, broiler, or flame to caramelize the top, like *crème brûlé*.

Buffet froid (BOO-fay fwah). A selection of dishes served cold or at room temperature.

Bugnes (bun-YUH). Sweet fritters. (See Regional/Seasonal Specialties: Burgundy and the Lyonnais.)

Cacahouètes (kah-kah-WHETT). Peanuts. This legume is not used very much in French cooking, but you will often find roasted, salted peanuts sold in snack-sized boxes at corner grocery stores and *tabac* shops. They may also be part of your hotel minibar selection.

Cacao (kah-kah-OH). Cocoa, usually referring to unsweetened powdered cocoa used for cooking.

(à la) (mode de) Caen (ah lah mode deh kah). Dishes prepared in the style of the Normandy town of Caen,

usually, a dish cooked in Calvados (dry apple brandy) and white wine and/or cider. (See also Regional/Seasonal Specialties: Normandy.)

Caille (KA-yee). Quail.

Calvados (KAL-vah-dohs). A region in Normandy famous for its apple brandy. The word "Calvados" also refers to the brandy itself, which is strong, clear distilled beverage made from apples. (See also Regional/Seasonal Specialties: Normandy and Beverages A to Z: After-Dinner Drinks.)

Camembert (KAM-uhm-bair). A small, circular, creamy, mild-tasting cheese from the village of Auge in Normandy. (See also Market Buying Tips: *Fromageries,* and Regional/Seasonal Specialties: Normandy.)

Camomille (KAH-mo-MEE-yuh). Camomile, an herb often used to make tea that is frequently taken after dinner to help induce sleep.

(à la) campagne (ah lah kahm-PAN-yah). Dishes prepared in a rustic or country style. The term is often used to describe pâté. (See Market Buying Tips: Meats.)

Canard (KAH-nard). Duck. Duck is a specialty of the Southwest, where the breasts—*magret* (mah-gray)— of fattened ducks are often served grilled.

Caneton (ka-neh-TOHN). Young male duck or duckling. This is the term usually used to describe duckling. The French roast it, stew it, and more. And remember that old American restaurant classic from the seventies, duck à l'orange? Well, you may find it on menus in traditional restaurants in France, and, when well prepared, it is quite delicious, not the sweet, sticky, greasy concoction many of us know.

Canette (ka-NETT). Young female duck or duckling.

Cannelle (ka-NELL). Cinnamon. This spice is often used to flavor desserts such as poached fruit or ice cream.

Cantal (kahn-TAHL). A large, cylindrical, firm cow's milk cheese made in the Auvergne region. (See also Market Buying Tips: *Fromageries.*)

Câpre (KA-pruh). Caper.

Carbonnade (KAHR-boh-NAHD). Literally, "glowing coals," referring to meats cooked over an open fire. The term can also refer to a stew of Flemish origin made with beef, beer, and onions.

Carotte (kah-ROTT). Carrot. Carrots are often served cooked as an accompaniment to roast meats, poultry, and fish. Carrots are also served raw in a salad called *carottes râpées* (kah-ROTT rah-PAY), which consists of julienned (cut into matchstick strips) carrots tossed with a vinaigrette dressing. It's a delicious salad for a picnic or lunch on the train.

Carré d'agneau (kah-RAY dan-YOH). Rack of lamb.

Carré de porc (kah-RAY deh por). Rack of pork.

Carré de veau (kah-RAY deh voh). Rack of veal.

Cary (kah-REE). Curry. Although curry is not a traditional seasoning in France, some contemporary chefs use it in innovative dishes.

Cassis (kah-SEES). Black currants, often used to make crème de cassis (KREHM deh kah-SEES), a black currant liqueur that can be sipped as an after-dinner drink but is most often mixed with dry white wine to make an apéritif known as *kir*.

Cassoulet (kah-soo-LAY). A stew famous in southwestern France made of white beans, plus sausages, pork, lamb, duck, and goose or a mixture of all or several of these meats. It is rich and hearty and can suffice as a meal, accompanied by only a glass or two of red wine, crusty bread, and a green salad. (See Regional/Seasonal Specialties: Languedoc.)

Cebiche or *seviche* (seh-BEESH or seh-VEESH). This term usually refers to raw fish marinated in citrus juices and seasonings.

Céleri (SEH-leh-REE). Celery. The type of celery most Americans are familiar with is called *céleri* or *céleri branche* (SEH-leh-REE bransh). Sometimes the word *céleri* is used to describe a root vegetable, *céleri-rave* or *celeriac* (see below).

Céleri-rave (SEH-leh-REE rahv) or *celeriac* (SEH-leh-ree-AK). Celery root, a root vegetable usually served julienned (cut into matchstick strips) and tossed in a rémoulade sauce, a spicy mayonnaise. It is a typical offering at most charcuteries in France.

Cèpe (sehp). A wild mushroom, known in Italy as porcini. Cèpes are beige to light brown in color and have a rich, meaty flavor. They are most abundant in the fall.

Cerfeuil (sehr-FOY). Chervil, a delicately flavored herb that is best used fresh since its flavors fade when cooked.

Cerise (seh-REES). Cherry. Fresh cherries are available in early summer in French markets. They are enjoyed fresh and in Alsace are used to make a strong, distilled brandy called *kirsch* (See Beverages A to Z: After-Dinner Drinks).

Cervelles (suhr-VELL). Brains, usually calf or lamb. Brains have a surprisingly delicate flavor, but, unfortunately, they *look* like what they are, and they are loaded with cholesterol. There are many food lovers, however, who adore brains, and if you do, you should try them in France.

Champignon (SHAM-pee-NYOHN). Mushroom. The term is usually used to refer to the little ivory-capped cultivated mushrooms, known in the States as "button mushrooms."

Chanterelle (SHAN-tuh-rell). A yellowish wild mushroom with a trumpet shape and fragrant flavor. Also known as *girolle* (jhee-ROHL).

Chantilly (SHAN-tee-yee). Whipped cream usually sweetened with sugar and flavored with vanilla. The traveler might see it listed on menus as *crème Chantilly*.

Charcuterie (SHAHR-koo-tuh-REE). Prepared meat products, usually pork, ham, sausages, or *rillettes*. Also, the place where you buy them. (See also Market Buying Tips: *Charcuteries*.)

Chardonnay (SHAR-duh-NAY). A grape that produces white wines and is used in making Champagne and Burgundies. (See also Beverages A to Z: Wine.)

Charlotte (shar-LOHT). A dessert consisting of custard poured into a mold lined with ladyfingers, then chilled and unmolded, served chilled. Or, a dish lined with buttered bread, filled with fruit, and baked, unmolded, and served warm.

Charolais (shar-oh-LAY). A region in Burgundy noted for its white cattle, which produce excellent beef. (See also Regional/Seasonal Specialties: Burgundy and the Lyonnais.)

Châtaigne (sha-TAN-yuh). Wild chestnut. The cultivated kind are known as *marrons*.

Châteaubriand (SHA-toh-bree-AHN). A thick filet steak, usually served with potatoes and a béarnaise sauce.

Chaud (shoh). Hot or warm.

Chaud-froid (shoh-FWAH). Literally, "hot cold." The term refers to a game or poultry dish that is served with a thick white sauce and aspic, served cold.

Chaudrée (shoh-DRAY). A fish stew, usually made with conger eel, white fish, potatoes, garlic, and wine. This is where we get the word "chowder."

Chausson (shoh-SOHN). Literally, "shoe." A savory or sweet turnover that is often filled with cooked fruit, such as apples.

Cheval (sheh-VAHL). Horse. In the market area, the traveler may see a shop that sells only horsemeat, a *boucherie chevaline*. Horsemeat is said to have a slightly sweet taste, but I cannot confirm this.

Cheveux d'ange (she-VOH dahnjh). Literally, "angel's hair," thin pasta, like angel-hair pasta in the U.S.A.

Chèvre (SHEHV-ruh). Goat, or cheese made from goat's milk. (See Market Buying Tips: *Fromageries.*)

Chevreau (shev-ROH). Young goat.

Chevreuil (shehv-ROY). Young roe buck, venison. The traveler is most likely to find venison on the menu in autumn and winter. The filet, often cut into noisettes, is prepared in a variety of ways, often grilled or sauteed with cherries, juniper berries, madeira sauce, or truffles.

Chicorée (sheh-koh-REE). Also known as *frisée*, this is a frizzy-leafed, mildly bitter salad green known as curly endive in English. It is often used in making a salad dressed with bacon and a warm dressing made from the bacon's pan drippings.

Chiffonnade (SHEH-fuh-NAHD). Cut into thin strips, especially herbs, lettuce, or sorrel.

Chocolat (SHOH-koh-LAH). Chocolate. (See Market Buying Tips: *Chocolateries.*)

Chocolat amer (SHOH-koh-LAH tah-MAIR). Bittersweet chocolate.

Chocolat au lait (SHOH-koh-LAH toh lay). Milk chocolate.

Chocolat chaud (SHOH-koh-LAH shoh). Hot chocolate. (See also Beverages A to Z: *Chocolat.*)

Chocolat mi-amer (SHOH-koh-LAH mee-ah-MAIR). Bittersweet chocolate that is sweeter than *chocolat amer*.

Choix (shwah). Choice. This word appears on menus when the diner has the option of choosing from several offerings.

Choron (sho-ROHN). Sauce combining béarnaise sauce and tomatoes.

Chou (plural *choux*) (both the singular and plural are pronounced "shoo"). Cabbage. The French work wonders with this humble vegetable, which is a particular specialty of Alsace and the mountainous regions of France. (See also Regional/Seasonal Specialties: Alsace-Lorraine.)

Chou de Bruxelles (SHOO deh brooks-ell). Brussels sprouts.

Choucroute (SHOO-kroot). Sauerkraut. (See also Regional/Seasonal Specialties: Alsace-Lorraine.)

Choucroute garnie (SHOO-kroot gar-NEE). Sauerkraut served with potatoes and a variety of meats. (See also Regional/Seasonal Specialties: Alsace-Lorraine.)

Chou-fleur (SHOO-fluhr). Cauliflower. This vegetable is sometimes served as a side dish to meats, poultry, and fish.

Choux, pâte à (pah-tah SHOO). A type of pastry used to make cream puffs, éclairs, *gougères,* and other sweet and savory pastries.

Ciboulette (SEE-boo-LETT). Chives.

Citron (sih-TROHN). Lemon.

Citron vert (sih-TROHN VAIR). Lime.

Civet (SEE-viht). A stew, usually made with game—especially hare—and thickened with blood.

Clafoutis (kla-foo-TEE). A rustic dessert made by topping a batter cake with fresh fruit, traditionally, black cherries.

Cochon (ko-SHON). Pig, pork.

Cochon de lait (ko-SHON deh lay). Suckling pig.

Coco (KO-ko). Coconut, also the name for a small white bean.

Coeur de palmier (KOOR deh PAL-mee-AY). Hearts of palm, usually served with vinaigrette dressing as a starter.

Complet (KOM-pleh). Booked, filled up. The term is used to describe a hotel or restaurant that is "full" and can take no more reservations.

Compris (kohm-PREE). Included, as in "service included."

Comté (KOHM-tay). A large, round cow's milk cheese made in the Jura mountains. (See also Market Buying Tips: *Fromageries.*)

Concassé (kohn-kah-SAY). Chopped, crushed. This term is often used to describe chopped, seeded, peeled tomatoes.

Concombre (kohn-KOHM-bruh). Cucumber.

Confiserie (kohn-FEE-sree). Confections, candy, or sweets. Or a shop that sells them. Chocolates are usually referred to separately, although there are chocolate shops (*chocolateries*) that sell both chocolate and nonchocolate candy. (See Market Buying Tips: *Chocolateries.*)

Confit (kohn-FEE). A kind of potted meat usually made with duck, goose, or pork. The meat is salted, then cooked and preserved in its own fat. The word "confit" is sometimes used to describe fruits preserved in sugar, alcohol, or vinegar. (See Regional/ Seasonal Specialties: The Pays Basque, Gascony, and the Pyrénées.)

Confiture (KOHN-fee-TUHR). Fruit jam or preserves. This is what you'll be served at breakfast to embellish your breads and croissants.

Consommation (KOHN-soh-mah-see-OHN). Literally, "consumption." The term refers to drinks, snacks, and meals that are served in a bar or café.

Consommé (KOHN-suh-may). A clear soup usually of beef, game, or poultry. This is a good word to know if you have a hangover, an upset stomach, or simply want something light and easy to digest.

Contre-filet (KOHN-truh fee-LAY). Part of the sirloin that lies above the loin, also known as *faux-filet*. A *contre-filet* can be roasted, braised, or grilled.

Coq au vin (KOH-koh VAHN). Chicken stewed in red wine, with bacon, pearl onions, and mushrooms. This dish is deeply flavored and is a particular specialty of Burgundy, but cooks in Alsace prepare it, too, using the local wine Riesling. (See Regional/Seasonal Specialties: Burgundy and Alsace-Lorraine.)

Coquillage(s) (KOH-kee-YAJH). Shellfish. This is an important word to know if you're allergic to this family of foods.

Coquille Saint-Jacques (koh-KEEL sahn-JHAHK). Sea scallops. These are often served in France with the roe, which is very rich. If you are sensitive to rich foods, skip the roe or take an antacid.

Coriandre (KOH-ree-AHN-druh). Coriander. This usually refers to the spice, not the herb.

Cornichon (KOR-nee-SHON). Small pickles, gherkins. These tangy-sweet, crunchy little pickles are often served with pâté.

Côte (kote). Rib, as in beef rib. Also refers to chops, which, of course, incorporate the rib.

Côte d'agneau (kote dan-YO). Lamb chops.

Côte de boeuf (kote deh BUHF). Beef rib steak.

Côte de veau (kote deh VO). Veal chop.

Côtelette (KOH-teh-LETT). A thin chop or cutlet of veal, lamb, or mutton.

Cotriade (KOH-tree-AHD). The local fish stew of Brittany. (See Regional/Seasonal Specialties: Brittany.)

Coulis (koo-LEE). Puree of raw or cooked fruit or vegetables. A *coulis* can be sweet or savory and is served as a kind of sauce to accompany desserts as well as savory dishes.

Courgette (koor-JHETT). Zucchini.

Crabe (krahb). Crab.

Crème (krehm). Cream. Cream is used a great deal in French cooking. Taste it, and you'll see why! The French don't generally substitute lower-fat dairy products for cream because—even though they're watching their weight more than ever before—they believe in using traditional ingredients. So how do they keep their weight down? They tend to eat smaller portions than Americans do.

Crème anglaise (KREHM ahn-GLEHZ). A sweetened, vanilla-flavored custard sauce often served with fruit desserts.

Crème brûlée (KREHM broo-LAY). A rich custard dessert with a brittle, caramelized topping.

Crème caramel (KREHM kai-rah-MEHL). A baked custard, served chilled with a thin, syrupy, transluscent caramel sauce. This is a classic French dessert and, when well prepared, an example of how simple ingredients can be made into something extraordinary. Traveling with children? They'll love this nursery dessert.

Crème fraîche (krehm FRESH). A thick, tangy cream, similar to sour cream. This luscious ingredient has been the downfall of many a disciplined dieter visiting France.

Crémets (kray-MEH). A fresh, mild cheese sometimes eaten for dessert. (See Regional/Seasonal Specialties: The Loire and Market Buying Tips: *Fromageries.)*

Crêpe (krehp). A large, thin pancake served with either sweet or savory accompaniments. (See Regional/Seasonal Specialties: Brittany.)

Cresson (kreh-SOHN). Watercress.

Crevette (kreh-VEHT). Shrimp.

Croissant (KWAH-sahn). A flaky, buttery, crescent-shaped pastry.

Croque-madame (KROHK-mah-DAHM). An open-faced sandwich of ham and cheese with an egg on top. This sandwich is offered at most cafés throughout the country.

Croque-monsieur (KROHK muh-SYUR). A toasted ham and cheese sandwich. Like *Croque-madame*, this sandwich is available at most cafés in France. This is the perfect lunch if you're traveling with a child who will only eat grilled cheese sandwiches.

Croustade (kroo-STAHD). A double-crust tart. (See Regional/Seasonal Specialties: The Pays Basque, Gascony, and the Pyrénées.)

Cru (kroo). Raw.

Crudités (KROO-dee-tay). Raw vegetables cut into bite-sized pieces and accompanied by a dipping sauce. They are usually served as an hors d'oeuvre.

Crustacé (KROO-sta-say). Crustacean. Know how to say this word if you are allergic to shellfish. Or if you want to eat it.

Cuisse (kwees). Leg or thigh, usually used to describe poultry.

Cuit (kwee). Cooked.

Daube (dohb). A stew of beef, lamb, mutton, or poultry usually made with red wine, onions, and tomatoes. Daubes are hearty, earthy dishes that are particularly satisfying in cool weather.

Daurade (doh-RAHD). Sea bream, also known as *dorade*.

Dégustation (DAY-goo-STAH-see-on). Tasting or sampling. This word is used to describe a menu offering many courses at a set price.

Déjeuner (DAY-jhuh-NAY). Lunch.

Demi (DEH-mee). Half. This word can be used to describe a portion that is smaller — or half the size — of the original. It is also part of the description of the dish *poularde en demi-deuil* (poo-LAHRD on deh-

MEE doy) or "chicken in half mourning." This dish is so called because the sliced truffles under the chicken's skin give it a slightly gray appearance.

Demi-glace (deh-mee GLAHS). Literally, "half-glaze," a rich, brown, meat-based reduction used to make sauces. The *demi-glace* gives the sauce a complex, concentrated flavor.

Dents-de-lion (DEHN-deh-lee-OHN). Dandelion greens, also known as *pissenlit*, which means "pee in the bed," referring to the greens' diuretic properties. The greens are tastiest in spring when they're young and tender. They are often served as a salad with a warm dressing.

Désossé (DAY-soh-SAY). Boned. The word is used to describe chicken or any meat or fish that has had its bones removed.

Dessert (deh-SAIR). Dessert.

(à la) Diable (ah lah dee-AH-bluh). Literally, "devil's style," meat or poultry that is prepared or served with a sauce of mustard, vinegar, and/or other pepper-based flavorings. The word is obviously a reference to the spicy-hot nature of the sauce.

(à la) Dijonnaise (ah lah DEE-zho-NAYZ). In the style of Dijon, usually with mustard sauce. (See Regional/Seasonal Specialties: Burgundy and the Lyonnais.)

Dinde (dand). Turkey hen.

Dindon (dan-DOHN). Turkey cock.

Dindonneau (DAN-doh-NOH). Young turkey.

Dîner (DEE-nay). Dinner.

Doré (doh-RAY). Golden brown.

Doux, douce (the masculine form is pronounced "doo," the feminine form is pronounced "doos"). Sweet.

Dragées (drah-JHAY). Sugared almonds. You'll find these at confiseries and specialty foods shops.

Duxelles (dooks-ELL). Minced mushrooms and shallots sautéed in butter, then mixed with cream. *Duxelles* are not served alone as a side dish but are used in the preparation of other foods, as in stuffings for meats and poultry.

Écrevisse (AY-kreh-VEES). Freshwater crayfish.

Émincé (AY-man-SAY). Thin slice. This is a good word to know when shopping at a cheese shop or charcuterie.

Emmenthal (EH-mahn-TAHL). A cow's milk cheese produced in the Jura mountains. (See Market Buying Tips: *Fromageries*.)

Encre (AHNK-ruh). Squid or octopus ink. If you like blood sausage, tripe, and other foods with strong, earthy flavors, you'll probably like octopus ink, which is sometimes used to flavor pasta.

Endive (ahn-DEEV). Belgian endive. This pale green, wonderfully crunchy vegetable is enjoyed raw in salads as well as braised and in gratins.

Entrecôte (AHN-treh-KOHT). Beef rib steak, often served with *frites,* or French fries.

Entrée (ahn-TRAY). The word means "entry." In culinary terms, technically the word refers to the course that precedes the meat course. At formal dinners, the entrée is served between the fish course and the meat course. Such dishes might include foie gras (served hot or cold), a terrine of poultry, game, or vegetables, quenelles made of poultry, sweetbreads, kidneys, or brains.

Épaule (AY-pahl). Shoulder, usually referring to shoulder of veal, lamb, mutton, or pork.

Épice (AY-pees). Spice.

Épinard (AY-pee-NAHR). Spinach. This green vegetable is often served cloaked with butter and/or cream. Your kids still won't like it.

Escalope (EH-ska-LOHP). Thin slice of meat or fish. Because this cut is thin, it is usually cooked very quickly, either in a sauté pan or on the grill.

Escargots (ESS-kar-GOH). Snails, usually served with butter, garlic, and parsley. They are a specialty of Burgundy, and the best are said to be a type called *petit gris* (peh-tee gree), "little gray." (See Regional/Seasonal Specialties: Burgundy and the Lyonnais.)

Espadon (ESS-pah-dohn). Swordfish.

(à l') Espagnole (ah lehs-pahn-YOLE). Literally, "Spanish style," foods prepared or served with tomatoes, bell peppers, onions, and garlic. This term often refers to a sauce with these ingredients.

Estragon (ESS-trah-GOHN). Tarragon. This pungent herb is handled deftly by French chefs, who understand that a little goes a long way. Tarragon is an especially good flavoring for simply prepared chicken.

Étouffé (AY-too-FAY). Stuffed. The term is not used to describe someone's state of being after a big meal but, rather, foods that can be stuffed, such as eggplant and zucchini.

(a l') Étouffée (ah l'AY-too-FAY) Literally, "smothered," foods that are cooked in a tightly closed pot

over low heat. The foods cook in their own juices, since in a "smothered" preparation there is very little liquid added.

Faisan (fay-SAHN). Pheasant. An elegant game bird with a mildly woodsy taste. It is most often seen on menus in autumn and winter.

Farci (far-SEE). Stuffed, as in stuffed game hens or chickens. If you feel "stuffed" after eating a big meal, do not say you are *farci*.

Faux-filet (FOH-fee-LAY). Part of the sirloin, also known as *contre-filet*.

Fenouil (fen-OO-yee). Fennel, the vegetable. This refreshing, crunchy vegetable has the consistency of celery and a mild anise flavor.

Figue (feeg). Fig.

Filet (fee-lay). Filet of meat or fish.

Financier (FEE-nahn-see-AY). A tiny, buttery-rich cake flavored with almonds. It is often served at tea or after dessert with espresso.

Fines herbes (feenz EHRB). A mixture of finely chopped aromatic herbs. Although the mixture may vary, the classic combination is chervil, chives, parsley, and tarragon.

Fixe (feex). Fixed. The word is used on menus and in restaurants as *prix fixe*, which means "set price." A prix fixe menu is one in which several courses are offered at a set price.

Flageolet (FLAH-jhoh-LAY). A type of legume that ranges in color from pale green to ivory. It has a mild, earthy flavor and delicate texture and is a classic accompaniment to lamb.

Flambé (flahm-BAY). Flamed, usually, a food sprinkled with liquor and then ignited with a match.

Flamiche (flah-MEESH). A quichelike vegetable tart that is a specialty of northern France. (See Regional/Seasonal Specialties: Champagne, the North, and the Île de France.)

Flammekueche (FLAH-meh-KOOSH). A pizzalike tart topped with cheese, bacon, and onions. It's also called *tarte flambée* (tahrt flahm-BAY). (See Regional/Seasonal Specialties: Alsace-Lorraine.)

Flan (flahn). A custard that can be sweet or savory, such as a vegetable or goat cheese flan. Dessert flans are similar to classic egg custard. Order one if you want something smooth and comforting.

(à la) Florentine (ah lah FLO-rehn-TEEN). Literally, "Florentine style," dishes served with spinach and a *Mornay* cheese sauce. The word "Florentine" can

also refer to a cookie studded with candied fruit and coated with chocolate.

Foie (fwah). Liver.

Foie gras (fwah grwah). Literally, "fat liver," liver from a goose or duck that has been force fed. The liver is cooked, then sliced and served hot or cold or made into pâté.

Fondu (fon-DOO). Melted, also, a thick cheese sauce for dipping vegetables or bread cubes. This rich, cholesterol-laden dish is delicious after a day of skiing on the French Alps.

(Au) four (oh foor). Baked or roasted in the oven.

Fraîche (fresh). Cool, fresh (feminine form).

Frais (freh). Cool, fresh (masculine form).

Fraise (frehz). Strawberry. This fruit is best in spring. The tiny little *fraise de bois* (frehz deh bwah), which are about the size of a child's thumbnail, are intensely flavored and difficult to find outside Europe. They are usually available only in May. If you see them on the menu, do order them.

Framboise (fram-bwaz). Raspberry. Freshly picked, this glorious berry is better than any hot house, mass-produced raspberry could ever be.

Fricassée (FREE-kah-SAY). A kind of stew, usually of chicken or veal, in a cream sauce. It's mildly flavored and rather old fashioned, but sometimes when you're traveling, that's exactly the kind of food you want.

Friture (free-TUHR). Tiny, deep-fried fish (usually whitebait or smelt) often served with apéritifs. (See Regional/Seasonal Specialties: The Loire.)

Froid (fwah). Cold, cool.

Fromage (FRO-majh). Cheese. France produces more different kinds of cheese than any other country in the world. (See Market Buying Tips: *Fromageries.*)

Fruit (fwee). Fruit. If you love fresh fruit but live in a place where most of the fruit is imported, indulge yourself in the luscious fruits of France. They are often organically grown and are generally picked closer to ripening time than some fruits in the U.S.A., which are picked green, then "ripen" while traveling to the marketplace. This means that in France, you will more than likely eat fruits soon after they're picked, when they are at their peak of flavor and texture.

Fruits de mer (FWEE deh MAIR). Seafood, usually referring to crustaceans and mollusks, not fish.

Fumé (foo-MAY). Smoked, cured. This term is used to describe ham, salmon, and other smoked or cured foods. It is also the word used in relation to cigarettes; *fumer* means to smoke.

Galette (gah-LEHT). A round, flat cake, tart, or pastry that can be either savory or sweet. Also, in Brittany another name for crêpes. (See Seasonal/Regional Specialties: Brittany.)

Garbure (gar-BUHR). A vegetable soup made with cabbage, *haricots*, garlic, herbs, and sometimes chestnuts. Preserved goose, duck, ham, pork, or turkey are also usually added. It is a rustic dish and may be found in country restaurants in the Pyrénées or the Pays Basque.

Garni (gahr-NEE). Garnished. The word is also used to describe sauerkraut with sausages. (See *Choucroute garnie* and Regional/Seasonal Specialties: Alsace-Lorraine.)

Garniture (GAHR-nee-TUHR). Garnish, often the vegetables that accompany a dish, such as peas, carrots, or broccoli florets.

(à la) Gasconne (ah lah gas-KOHN). Literally, "in the style of Gascony." (See also Regional/Seasonal Specialties: The Pays Basque, Gascony, and the Pyrénées.)

Gâteau (gah-toh). Cake. French cakes are more about fillings, glazes, and icings than the cake itself, which is quite the opposite of a traditional American layer cake, with its thick cake layers and mere half-inch of frosting. Both American and French cakes have their place in the world's repertoire of desserts.

gâteau Basque (gah-toh bahsk). A cake that has a sweet dough with a texture somewhere between cookie, pie crust, and cake and a rich pastry cream filling (and sometimes fruit).

gâteau opera (gah-toh oh-PAY-rah). An elaborate almond sponge cake embellished with coffee- and chocolate-flavored fillings. The word "opera" is traditionally written on the cake with icing.

Gaufre (GOH-frah). Waffle. Similar to American waffles, gaufres are often sold garnished with sugar and/or whipped cream at outdoor stands. (See Regional/Seasonal Specialties: Champagne, the North, and the Île de France.)

Gelée (jheh-LAY). Jelly, aspic. There are many French dishes that are served *en gelée*, that is, coated or covered with aspic. When it is properly made, aspic is sparkling and transluscent, nicely flavored, and delicate in texture. Aspic should not be cloudy or rubbery.

Gibier (JHEE-bee-AY). Game. This word can refer to both winged game as well as venison, hare, and their relatives.

Gigot (JHEE-goh). Hind leg of mutton or lamb.

Glace (glahs). Ice, ice cream. Ice is not automatically served with cold drinks in France, so if you want it, you may have to ask for it. The word *glace* also means ice cream. This is a beloved dessert in France and is offered at nearly every bistro, brasserie, and restaurant in the country. But don't expect to find as many flavors as you do in the States! French ice cream is usually full-fat, richly flavored, and all-natural.

Glacé (glah-say). Means "glazed" or "frozen," "iced" or "ice- cold" as in *marrons glacés*, which are candied chestnuts.

Gougére (goo-JHAIR). A savory, cheese-flavored pastry that is a specialty of Burgundy. (See Regional/Seasonal Specialties: Burgundy and the Lyonnais.)

(à la) Grand-mère (ah lah grwan mair). Literally, "grandmother's style," dishes prepared with onions, mushrooms, potatoes, and bacon. If you need some comforting, order anything from the menu labeled *grand-mere*.

Gratin (grah-TAHN). A dish cooked in the oven or under the broiler, sometimes topped with bread crumbs or cheese. *Gratins* are a particular specialty of Lyon. (See Regional/Seasonal Specialties: Burgundy and the Lyonnais.)

Gratin dauphinoise (grah-TAHN do-fee-NWAZ). Sliced potatoes baked with milk and cheese. (See Regional/Seasonal Specialties: Franche-Comté, Savoy, and the Dauphine.)

Grenouille (grah-NOO-ee). Frog. Most people who love frogs' legs say they taste like chicken. I say they taste like frogs' legs and to heck with them. On the menu, they'll be listed as *cuisses de grenouille* (kwees deh grah-NOO-ee).

Gribiche (greh-BEESH). A vinaigrette sauce with the addition of chopped hard-boiled egg yolks, gherkins, and capers. It's often served with cold fish.

Grillade (gree-YAHD). Grill, cooked on the grill. This can refer to meats or vegetables.

Gros sel (GRO sel). Coarse salt. There are several traditional dishes cooked in coarse salt, particularly whole chicken or fish. The salt seals in the flavors of the poultry or fish without imparting a salty taste. When it is served, the waiter cracks open the salt crust and serves the moist, steaming chicken or fish. This is a good choice for calorie watchers; just ask the waiter to hold the sauce.

Hareng (ai-RAHNG). Herring.

Haricot (AH-ree-KOH). Bean. This word is most often used to describe the very thin young green beans called *haricots verts* (AH-ree-KOH VAIR).

Herbe (airb). Literally, "grass." Also, kitchen herbs or potherbs.

Hollandaise (oh-luhn-DEHZ). A rich, warm sauce of butter, egg yolks, and lemon juice often served with fish, eggs, and vegetables.

Homard (OH-mahr). Lobster. If you love plain, boiled Maine lobster with nothing more than melted butter, you may find French lobster dishes too fussy. For example, *homard à l'américaine* is sautéed lobster with white wine, brandy, garlic, shallots, tomatoes, and butter.

Huile (wheel). Oil.

Huître (WHEE-truh). Oyster. The French love oysters, and it is recommended that you try them if you also love them. They are often served raw as an appetizer or warm, swathed in butter or cream. (See also Regional/Seasonal Specialties: Brittany and The Southwest.)

Jambon (jham-BOHN). Ham. (See Market Buying Tips: *Charcuteries*.)

(à la) jardinière (ah lah JHAR-dih-NAIR). Literally, "in the style of the gardener's wife," dishes prepared or served with mixed vegetables. Look for this term if you are craving veggies.

Julienne (jhu-LYEHN). Matchstick strips. Almost any firm vegetable can be cut into julienne strips. To make them at home, you can use a sharp, heavy knife, but the julienne attachment to the food processor makes this an easier task.

Jus (jhoo). Juice. This word can refer to fruit juice, as in *jus d'orange*, or meat juices, which are often served as a light, natural sauce. Sautéed chops or lamb chops, for example, might be served *au jus* (oh jhoo); that is, with cooking juices from the sauté pan.

Kugelhopf (KOO-guhl-HOPF). A light yeast cake with nuts and dried fruit. (See Regional/Seasonal Specialties: Alsace-Lorraine.)

Lait (lay). Milk. The French do not drink much milk as a beverage, and it is not often served in restaurants, except perhaps to children. If you order milk with your morning cereal or porridge, it will probably be whole milk. If you want low-fat milk, ask for *lait écremé* (LAY-tay kreh-MAY), but your request may not be fulfilled except in very large, tourist-driven hotels.

Laitue (lah-TOO). Lettuce.

(à la) Landaise (ah lah lahn-DAYZ). In the style of Landes, an area in the Southwest, prepared or served with

goose fat, garlic, pine nuts, and/or Armagnac. (See also Regional/Seasonal Specialites: The Southwest.)

Langoustine (LAHN-goo-STEEN). Scampi, prawn.

Langue (lawng). Tongue. If you've never been able to bring yourself to cook beef tongue, do try it in France if you have the opportunity. It tastes somewhat like corned beef.

Lapin (lah-PAN). Rabbit. Rabbit is frequently prepared with mustard sauce. Try not to think about its cute little face. Concentrate instead on the fact that it is a pure, lean food, with no preservatives and almost no fat. There. Don't you feel better?

Lardon (lahr-DOHN). Bacon. This is not really served as it is in the States but instead is diced and used in cooking.

Légumes (lay-GOOM). Vegetables. Sometimes vegetables must be ordered à la carte. If you're craving roughage, don't expect a big side dish of veggies necessarily to accompany your roast chicken.

Lentilles (lahn-TEE). Lentils. These are handled with reverence in most areas of France, especially in Le Puy, where they are a specialty. (See Regional/ Seasonal Specialties: Central France.)

Limon (LEE-mohn). Lime. Also called *citron vert*.

Lotte (lot). Monkfish, anglerfish.

Loup de mer (LOO deh mair). Sea bass.

(à la) Lyonnaise (ah lah LEE-oh-NAYZ). In the style of Lyons, dishes prepared or served with onions. *Pommes de terre lyonnaise* (pohm deh tair LEE-oh-NAYZ), sautéed potatoes with onions, is a traditional *lyonnaise* dish. (See also Regional/Seasonal Specialties: Burgundy and the Lyonnais.)

Macaron (MAH-ka-ROHN). Macaroon. French macaroons are not thick, dense globs of coconut; they are light, crunchy perfections made of egg whites, sugar, and almonds.

Mâche (mahsh). Known in English as lamb's lettuce, corn salad, or field salad, this tender, leafy green is delightful on its own dressed with a simple vinaigrette or mixed with other delicate salad greens.

Madeleines (MAH-dah-LAHN). Small, shell-shaped sponge cakes originally from Commercy in Lorraine.

(à la) Madrilène (ah lah MAD-ruh-LEHN). In the style of Madrid, foods that are cooked or flavored with tomatoes.

Magret (MAH-gray). Fillet, breast, usually of force-fed duck. Magret is a tender, flavorful cut, often cooked rare or medium rare.

Maïs (maze). Corn. Many old-time French chefs laugh at the way Americans eat corn, a vegetable they consider "animal food." Americans may have the last laugh, however, because more and more young French chefs are featuring tender sweet corn on their menus, not as corn on the cob, but in sophisticated vegetable stews and composed salads.

Mangue (mahng). Mango.

Marron (mah-ROHN). Cultivated chestnut, derived from the wild *châtagne*. During the autumn months, the traveler may see fresh chestnuts in the market as well as candied chestnuts—*marrons glacées* (mah-ROHN glah-SAY)—in candy shops and chocolate shops. (See also Regional/Seasonal Specialties: Languedoc.)

Matelote (MAH-teh-loht). A fish stew. (See Regional/Seasonal Specialties: The Loire.)

Médaillon (meh-DAHL-yuhn). A round or oval cut of meat, usually beef, veal, or pork. It is usually a crosswise cut from the filet.

Mélange (meh-LAHNJH). Mixture. The word might be used to describe a mixture of vegetables, served as a side dish.

Menthe (mahnt). Mint, the herb.

Merlan (mehr-LAHN). Whiting, the fish.

Merveilleuse (MEHR-vay-YUHZ). Sweet fritters flavored with Cognac. (See Regional/Seasonal Specialties: The Southwest.)

Mesclun (mess-KLAHN). Mixed young salad greens. The word *mesclun* comes from an old Provençal word meaning "mixed" and, in this case, refers to the many kinds of lettuce that make up the salad.

(à la) meunière (ah lah muh-NYAIR). Literally, "in the style of the miller's wife," usually fish dusted in flour, sautéed in butter, and served with browned butter, lemon juice, and parsley.

Meurette (myuh-RETT). Red wine sauce with onions, carrots, bacon, and mushrooms. It is often served with eggs in Burgundy. (See Regional/Seasonal Specialties: Burgundy and the Lyonnais.)

Miel (mee-YELL). Honey. The French have a thing for honey, and you'll find a variety of flavors on the shelves of a good specialty food store. Lavender and rosemary are only two of the many to look for. (Honeys make great gifts, too.)

Mijoté (mee-jho-TAY). Simmered.

(à la) Milanaise (ah lah MEE-lah-NEHZ). In the style of Milan, referring to food dipped in egg, then a mixture of bread crumbs and cheese, then fried.

Mille-feuille (meel-FOYEE). Literally, "thousand leaf," thin layers of puff pastry served with a sweet or savory filling or topping.

Mimosa (mee-MOH-zah). A garnish of chopped hard-boiled egg yolk.

Minceur (mahn-SUHR). Low-fat or low-calorie.

(à la) minute (ah lah mee-NOOT). From the English "minute," the term refers to beef or fish that is simply grilled or sautéed quickly and served with lemon juice and parsley.

Mirabelle (mee-ruh-BEHL). Small plum. Also, a clear, distilled spirit made from mirabelle plums.

(à la) mode (ah lah mode). "In the manner of." (See *Boeuf à la mode.)*

Mont-blanc (MAWN-blahn). Dessert of pureed chestnuts topped with whipped cream named for the peak Mont Blanc. It's an old-fashioned dessert but a must if you like chestnuts, which, by the way, are not botanically "nuts" but fruits. (See *Marron* and Regional/Seasonal Specialties: Languedoc.)

Morille (moh-REE). Morel, an edible wild mushroom that makes its appearance in the spring. Morels have a rather spongy texture and pleasant, earthy flavor.

Mornay (mor-NAY). A béchamel sauce with cheese added.

Morue (mo-ROO). Salt cod.

Moule (mool). Mussel.

Mousse (moos). Literally, "froth" or "foam," a sweet or savory dish, with egg whites or whipped cream, served hot or cold. The most famous, of course, is chocolate mousse, *mousse au chocolat* (moo-soh SHOH-koh-LAH).

Moutarde (moo-TAHRD). Mustard. Most of the mustard you'll be served in France will be the spicy, ocher-colored mustard of Dijon. It is usually served with sausages and is an ingredient in some sauces. (See Regional/Seasonal Specialties: Burgundy and the Lyonnais.)

Mouton (MOO-tohn). Sheep, mutton.

Mûre (muhr). Blackberry. This is a popular fruit used for making preserves—*confiture* (kohn-fee-TUHR)—for spreading on toast and breakfast breads.

Muscade (moo-SKOHD). Nutmeg. This spice is used to flavor many kinds of desserts.

(à la) Nage (ah lah NAJH). Literally, "swimming." The term usually refers to shellfish poached in an aromatic liquid of white wine, shallots, and herbs.

Napoléon (NAH-poh-lee-OHN). A layered dessert made with puff pastry and pastry cream, glazed with icing or dusted with sugar.

Nature (na-TUHR). Plain, without sauces, fillings, or other embellishments. This term is often used to describe such dishes as plain omelettes and plain vegetables.

Navarin (nah-vah-RAN). A stew of lamb or mutton with potatoes and onions.

Navet (na-VAY). Turnip. Cooked turnips are a traditional accompaniment to roast duck.

(à la) Niçoise (ah lah nee-SWAZ). Literally, "in the style of Nice," foods prepared or served with tomatoes, garlic, anchovies, olives, and capers. (See also Regional/Seasonal Specialties: Provence.)

Noisette (nwah-ZET). Hazelnut, also a small steak, usually of lamb or veal.

Noix (nwah). Nuts, usually walnuts. Also, the top side of veal.

(à la) Normande (ah lah nor-MAHND). Literally, " in the Normandy style," dishes prepared or served with cream and/or apples, apple cider, and Calvados, a clear, distilled spirit made from apples. (See also Regional/Seasonal Specialties: Normandy.)

Nougat (noo-GAH). A confection made of roasted nuts plus sugar or honey. (See Regional/Seasonal Specialties: Provence.)

Nouilles (NOO-ee). Long, flat noodles.

Oeuf (uhf). Egg. (Besides those listed below, see also Comfort Foods.)

- *Oeufs brouillés* (UH broo-YAY). Scrambled eggs. French scrambled eggs are cooked slowly over very low heat with butter and are generally softer and richer than American scrambled eggs.
- *Oeufs à la coque* (UH ah lah KOHK). Soft-cooked eggs.
- *Oeufs durs* (UH dur). Hard-boiled eggs.
- *Oeufs frits* (UH fwee). Fried eggs.
- *Oeufs en meurette* (UH sahn myu-RETT). Eggs poached with red wine, mushrooms, bacon, and baby onions. (See Regional/Seasonal Specialties: Burgundy and the Lyonnais.)
- *Oeufs mollets* (UH mo-YAY). Soft-boiled eggs.

- *Oeufs sur la plat* (UH sur lah PLAH). Eggs cooked in butter and served in a shallow baking dish.
- *Oeufs pochés* (UH po-SHAY). Poached eggs.

Oie (wah). Goose. This richly flavored dark-fleshed bird is a specialty of southwestern France. (See Regional/Seasonal Specialties: The Southwest.)

Oignon (on-YON). Onion. Some dishes prepared with or served with onions are described as *soubise*, as in *sauce soubise*.

Olive (oh-LEEV). Olive. Olives are a specialty of southern France, particularly Nice, where the local niçoise olives are a favorite. (See Regional/Seasonal Specialties: Provence.)

Omelette (ahm-LETT). Omelette, a mixture of eggs and seasonings with various fillings, cooked in a skillet.

Onglet (ohn-GLAY). Flank of beef, usually grilled with shallots.

Opéra (oh-PAY-rah). Literally, "opera." Refers to savory dishes prepared or served with chicken livers and asparagus tips. Also, *gâteau opéra*, an elaborate almond sponge cake embellished with coffee- and chocolate-flavored fillings. You'll recognize it in the pâtisserie, where the word "opera" is traditionally written on the cake with icing.

Orange (oh-RAHNJH). Orange.

Ordinaire (OHR-din-AIR). Ordinary, plain, as in *vin ordinaire* (va-nor-di-NAIR), a term used to describe plain, or everyday, wines.

Oreille (or-AYE). Ear, of a pig or calf. If you like pigs' feet and such, you'll be fine with pigs' ears.

Oseille (oh-ZAY). Sorrel, a spinachlike, leafy vegetable that has a tangy, lemony taste. It is often served with fish or with scrambled eggs.

Oursin (uhr-SAHN). Sea urchin. The coral (ovaries) is served either raw with lemon juice or added to scrambled eggs. *Oursin* is very rich and has a slight perfumy aroma. It is definitely a love-it-or-hate-it item.

Paillasson (pay-yah-SOHN). Literally, "doormat." *Pommes de terre paillasson* (pohm deh TAIR pa-yah-SOHN) or *pomme paille* (pohm pay-ee) are flat potato pancakes thought to resemble a woven doormat. They are usually served as a side dish, but some chefs make tiny pancakes, top them with *crème fraîche* and caviar, and serve them as hors d'oeuvres.

Paille (pay-EE). Literally, "straw." (See *Paillasson*.)

Pain (pan). Bread. (Besides those listed below, see also Market Buying Tips: *Boulangeries.*)

- *Pain complet* (PAN kohm-PLEH). Whole-wheat bread.
- *Pain d'épice* (pan day-PEES). Spice bread.
- *Pain de gênes* (PAN deh JHEN). A rich, almond-flavored sponge cake. (See Regional/Seasonal Specialties: Alsace-Lorraine.)
- *Pain grillé* (PAN gree-YAY). Toast, or grilled bread.
- *Pain de mie* (PAN de MEE). Sandwich bread, usually firm, white loaves, thinly sliced.
- *Pain perdu* (PAN pare-DOO). French toast.
- *Pain de siègle* (PAN de see-EGG-la). Rye bread.

Palmier (pahlm-YAY). Literally, "palm tree." A crisp, cookie-type sweet made of puff pastry whose shape is said to resemble a palm leaf. Also, *coeur de palmier* (koor de pahlm-YAY), hearts of palm, which is often served as a kind of salad with vinaigrette sauce.

Palourde (pah-LOORD). Clam.

Pamplemousse (PAHM-pluh-moose). Grapefruit.

Panaché (pah-nuh-SHAY). Mixed or variegated. In culinary terms, the word might be used to describe a dessert platter featuring many different kinds of sweets or a salad with many ingredients.

Pan bagna (pan BAHN-yah). A sandwich popular in southern France that is made with a long, flat loaf of bread or a roll, split and brushed with olive oil and filled with ingredients like onions, anchovies, black olives, and peppers. (See Regional/Seasonal Specialties: Provence.)

Pané (pa-NAY). Breaded, coated in bread crumbs.

Papillote (pa-pee-YOTE). Paper or aluminum foil packet in which fish, meat, and/or vegetables are sealed and baked. If you're watching your calories, anything cooked *en papillote* will probably be light and served with natural juices and no sauce.

Paquette (pa-KETT). Female lobster with its eggs.

Parfait (par-FAY). Literally, "perfect." Usually, the term refers to a rich, creamy frozen custard dessert.

Paris-Brest (PAH-ree brest). A classic dessert consisting of a ring of pastry filled with butter cream and almonds. This is a rather old-fashioned dessert but a rich and tasty one.

(à la) Parisienne (ah lah pa-REE-see-AHN). Literally, "in the Parisian style," usually, fish or chicken garnished with mushrooms, asparagus, truffles, and a white wine sauce.

Parmentier (PAR-mun-tee-AY). An economist and food writer who convinced the French to eat potatoes at a time when they were thought to be poisonous. The term is used to describe dishes with potatoes, e.g., *potage parmentier* (poh-tahjh PAR-mun-tee-AY), potato and leek soup.

Pastis (pass-TEES). The name of a certain type of double-crust tart. Also, licorice-flavored drink served as an apéritif. (See also Beverages A to Z: *Apéritifs*, and Regional/Seasonal Specialties: Pays Basque, Gascony, and the Pyrénées.)

Pâte (paht). A word used to refer to pastry, batter, paste, or dough. It also means pasta.

Pâté (pah-TAY). A mixture of meats, usually pork plus spices and herbs, baked in an earthenware baking dish (called a "terrine" both in French and in English) and usually eaten cool or at room temperature. (Besides those listed below, see also Market Buying Tips: *Charcuteries.*)

- *Pâté de campagne* (pah-TAY deh kahm-PAN-yah). A rather coarse, slightly crumbly, country-style meat loaf usually made with pork. It is usually served with mustard and gherkins.
- *Pâté en croûte* (pah-TAY-on-KROOT). *Pâté* that has been baked in a savory pastry crust.

Pâtisserie (PAH-tee-suh-REE). Pastries, cakes, and other baked sweets. Also, a shop selling these items. (See also Market Buying Tips: *Patisseries.*)

Paupiette (POH-pee-YETT). Usually, a thin slice of beef, veal, or sole that has been stuffed, rolled, and braised.

Pavé (pah-VAY). Literally, "cobblestone." A square or rectangular dessert, often a very rich chocolate confection called *pavé au chocolat* (pah-VAY oh shoh-koh-LAH).

(à la) Paysanne (ah lah PAY zann). Literally, "peasant-style," foods prepared or served with vegetables, usually carrots, onions, and ham.

Pêche (pesh). Peach.

Pêcheur (pesh-UHR). Literally, "fisherman." Refers to dishes made or served with fish and/or shellfish.

Perdreau (pare-DROH). Young partridge.

Perdrix (pare-DREE). Mature partridge.

(à la) Périgourdine (ah lah pair-eh-gor-DEEN). In the style of the Perigord in southwestern France. Also, foods prepared or served with truffles and/or foie gras. (See also Regional/Seasonal Specialties: The Southwest.)

Périgueux (pai-ree-GOH). Usually, a sauce made with Madeira and truffles. (See Regional/Seasonal Specialties: The Southwest.)

Persil (pair-SEE). Parsley.

Petit déjeuner (peh-TEE DAY-jhuh-NAY). Breakfast.

Petits fours (peh-tee FOOHR). Very small, bite-sized, sweet biscuits, cakes, or pastries, often served at the end of a meal.

Petit-pois (peh-tee PWAH). Small, young green peas.

Pétoncle (pay-TOHNK-luh). A small scallop.

Pichet (pee-SHAY). Jug or pitcher often used to serve water or table wine.

Pigeon (PEE-jhohn). Pigeon.

Pigeonneau (pee-jhohn-OH). Squab, young pigeon.

Pignons (de pin) (PEE-nyon deh-PAN). Pine nuts.

Piment (PEE-mahn). Pepper, referring to capsicum, the vegetable, not black pepper, the spice. Sweet peppers (bell peppers) are called *piment doux* (PEE-mahn DOO). Red peppers are used prolifically in Basque cooking. (See Regional/Seasonal Specialties: The Pays Basque, Gascony, and the Pyrénées.)

Piment doux (PEE-mahn DOO). Sweet bell pepper.

Pinot noir (PEE-noh NWAHR). A red grape that produces red Burgundy wines and often goes into making champagne. (See also Beverages A to Z: Wines.)

Pintade (pan-TODD). Guinea fowl.

Pipérade (PEE-pay-ROD). A mixture of tomatoes, peppers, and onions from the Basque region. (See Regional/Seasonal Specialties: The Pays Basque, Gascony, and the Pyrénées.)

Piquant (pee-KAHN). Spicy, piquant, pungent. *Sauce piquante* is a mixture of white wine, vinegar, shallots, capers, gherkins, and tarragon often served with sliced meats.

Pissaladière (pee-sa-LA-dee-YAIR). A pizzalike tart that is a specialty of southern France. This open-faced flat pie is usually topped with onion, anchovies, black olives, and sometimes tomatoes. (See Regional/Seasonal Specialties: Provence.)

Pistache (PEE-stash). Pistachio nut.

Pistou (PEE-stoo). A pungent sauce of basil, garlic, and olive oil that is a French adaptation of the Italian pesto sauce. It is often served with a vegetable soup and is stirred in just before serving. The dish is called *soupe au pistou* (soop oh PEE-stoo). (See Regional/Seasonal Specialties: Provence.)

Pithiviers (pee-TEE-vee-AY). A rich puff pastry dessert filled with almond- and rum-flavored cream.

Plat (plah). A word meaning "dish," both figuratively and literally, as in *plat du jour* (PLAH doo JHOOR) and *sur le plat* (SUHR lah PLAH), which means cooked in a shallow dish and served in the same dish.

Plat du jour (PLAH doo JHOOR). Specialty of the day.

Pleurote (plu-ROTT). A family of fungi that includes the oyster mushroom. These earthy little morsels have a woodsy flavor and are found most often in autumn.

Poché (po-SHAY). Poached, simmered gently in lightly bubbling water or other liquid. Dieters' alert: Look for the word *poché* on the menu so you can spend your calorie allotment on dessert.

Pochouse (po-SHOOSE) or *pochause*. A stew made with freshwater fish, usually eel, lotte, and bream, flavored with garlic and white wine. *Pochouse* is a specialty of Dijon, in the Burgundy region. (See also Regional/Seasonal Specialties: Burgundy and the Lyonnais.)

Poêle (pwal). Stove, frying pan; for example, *oeufs à la poêle*: fried eggs.

Poêlé(-e) (pwal-AY). Meats roasted on a bed of vegetables.

À point (ah PWAHN). Medium rare. The French tend to eat their meat a tad on the rare side, so be advised that chops, steaks, or fish cooked medium rare in France might be pinker than you would have in a restaurant in the States. *À point* can also refer to cheese or fruit that is perfectly ripe, at a good stage for eating.

Poire (pwahr). Pear.

Poire belle Hélène (pwahr bell ay-LAIN). A classic dessert consisting of poached pears with vanilla ice cream and chocolate sauce.

Poireau (plural *poireaux*) (both the singular and the plural are pronounced "pwah-ROW"). Leek. Cooked leeks are often served cold with a vinaigrette sauce as a first course.

Pois (pwah). Peas.

Poisson (pwah-SOHN). Fish.

Poitrine (pwah-TREEN). Breast of lamb or veal. Also, beef brisket.

Poivrade (pwah-VRAD). A sauce that combines vinegar, marinade, and black pepper that is often served with hare or venison.

Poivre (Pwahv). Pepper, referring to black pepper, the spice.

Poivron (pwahv-ROHN). Sweet bell pepper, also called *piment doux*. Sweet bell peppers are a very prominent ingredient in Basque cooking. (See also Regional/Seasonal Specialties: The Pays Basque.)

Pommade (po-MAHD). A thick, smooth mixture.

Pomme (pohm). Apple. Also, short for *pomme de terre*.

Pommes de terre (POHM deh TAIR). Potatoes. (See also Comfort Foods: Potatoes.)

Porc (pohr). Pork.

Porcelet (POR-seh-LAY). Suckling pig.

Porchetta (por-KE-tah). Whole, young, stuffed pig, spit-roasted. A specialty of southern France. The word *porchetta* also means the same thing in Italian.

Porto (POR-to). Port.

(à la) Portugaise (ah lah POR-tu-GEHZ). Portuguese- style, foods prepared with or served with some or all of the following ingredients: tomatoes, shallots, herbs, mushrooms, peppers, zucchini, and rice.

Potable (poh-TAHB-luh). Drinkable, as in *eau potable*, drinkable water.

Potage (poh-TAJH). A thickened soup, as opposed to a clear *consommé*, bouillon, or broth.

Pot-au-crème (PO-toh-KREM), also *pot de crème* or *petit pot de crème*. A cold, creamy, puddinglike dessert flavored with vanilla, coffee, or chocolate, traditionally served in small cups.

Pot-au-feu (PO-toh-FUH). Similar to pot roast, beef simmered with vegetables. This is a soothing, simple dish. (See Comfort Foods: Stews.)

Potée (poh-TAY). A hearty soup made of meats and vegetables, usually salt pork, cabbage, beans or lentils, and sausage. (See Regional/Seasonal Specialties: Alsace-Lorraine.)

Potiron (POH-tee-ROHN). Pumpkin.

Poularde (poo-LAHRD). A roasting chicken, usually a fattened hen.

Poule (pool). Hen or fowl for stewing, as in *poule au pot* (pool oh poh), chicken poached with vegetables, a soothing, light dish, good for calorie watchers.

Poulet (poo-LAY). Young chicken; *poulet fermier/de grain*, free-range chicken.

Poulette (poo-LETT). Young chicken, pullet.

Poulpe (poolp). Octopus.

Poussin (poo-SAN). Young, small chicken. These are very tender and often roasted whole.

Pralin (praw-lan). Praline, a powdered or finely chopped mixture of crunchy caramel and toasted nuts used in cooking desserts and sometimes sprinkled on top of them.

(à la) Presse/Pressé (ah lah PRESS/pre-SAY). Pressed, squeezed, e.g., *citron pressé*, fresh-squeezed lemon juice.

Primeur (pree-muhr). Early spring vegetables and fruits.

(à la) Printanière (ah lah PRAN-tan-YAIR). Dishes cooked or served with spring vegetables.

Prix fixe (pree feeks). Fixed price, a term describing a menu offering several courses at a set price.

Profiterole (pro-FEE-te-ROLL). Cream puffs with a sweet or savory filling. A very traditional dessert is *profiterole au chocolat,* consisting of cream puffs served with ice cream and chocolate sauce.

(à la) Provençale (ah lah PRO-vahn-SAHL). In the style of Provence, foods prepared or served with tomatoes, garlic, and sometimes olives, eggplants, and anchovies. (See Regional/Seasonal Specialties: Provence.)

Prune (proon). Plum.

Pruneau (PROO-noh). Prune, dried plum.

Purée (pyu-RAY). Puree, a smooth, thick, creamy mixture.

Quatre-quarts (KAHTR-kar). Literally, "four quarters," pound cake made of equal portions of eggs, butter, flour, and sugar.

Quenelle (kweh-NELL). A light dumpling poached in water or broth. The most common are those made of chicken or pike.

Quetsch (kesh). A variety of plum. Also, a clear, distilled spirit made from *quetsch* plums.

Queue (de boeuf) (KYEW deh BUHF). Oxtail, usually braised in wine with bacon, onions, and chestnuts.

Quiche (keesh). A savory, open-faced custard tart that is a specialty of Lorraine in Alsace. *Quiche Lorraine* is made with bacon, eggs, cream, and sometimes cheese. (See Regional/Seasonal Specialties: Alsace-Lorraine.)

Rafraîchi (RA-fra-SHEE). Chilled, cool. The term is often used to refer to fresh fruit.

Ragoût (rah-GOO). A thick stew made of meat, poultry, or fish. (See Comfort Foods: Stews.)

Raie (ray). Ray, skate, often served *au beurre noir,* in browned butter sauce.

Raifort (ray-FOHR). Horseradish; *sauce raifort,* creamy horseradish sauce.

Raisin (ray-SAHN). Grape.

Raisin sec (RAY-sahn SEK). Raisin.

Râpé (rah-PAY). Grated or shredded, e.g., *carottes rapées,* grated carrots.

Ratatouille (RAH-tah-TOO-ee). A blend of eggplant, zucchini, onion, and tomatoes. (See Regional/Seasonal Specialties: Provence.)

Ravigote (rah-vee-GOTE). A spicy vinaigrette sauce made with some or all of the following: vinegar, white wine, mustard, gherkins, capers, and olive oil.

Reblochon (reh-blow-SHOHN). A round, smooth, ivory-colored cow's milk cheese. (See Market Buying Tips: *Fromageries.*)

Réchauffé (RAY-sho-FAY). Reheated, a dish made with cooked meat.

Régime (ray-JHEEM). Diet, or a healthful way of eating. Travelers will probably find it difficult to stay on their regime while in France, but if one eats as the French do—three meals a day and no snacking—it is possible to return home without an extra ounce of fat.

Réglisse (ray-GLEES). Licorice.

(à la) Reine (ah lah REHN). Literally, "in the queen's style," a preparation often connected to Louis XV's queen, who was famous for her love of food. The term *à la reine* usually refers to dishes with chicken or pureed chicken.

Reine de Saba (REHN deh SAH-bah). Literally, "Queen of Sheba," a cake flavored with chocolate and almonds.

Relais (reh-LAY). Literally, "relay or change of horses." The term refers to an inn or hotel.

Religieuse (reh-leejh-UHZ). Literally, "nun." In culinary terms, this is an elaborate dessert made of éclairs that is said to resemble a nun in her robes. The term also refers to a jam tart with a lattice topping.

Rémoulade (ray-moo-LAHD). A tangy mayonnaise-based sauce seasoned with mustard, gherkins, capers, herbs, and anchovies that is often served with cold meats and fish.

Réveillon (REH-veh-yon). Late supper eaten on Christmas Eve and New Year's Eve.

Rhubarbe (roo-barb). Rhubarb.

Rhum (rum). Rum.

Riche (reesh). Literally, "rich." The word can be used to describe foods or dishes that are opulent, decadent, and/or caloric.

(à la) Richelieu (ah lah REESH-luh). Literally, "in the style of Cardinal Richelieu," foods garnished with stuffed tomatoes, mushrooms, braised lettuce, and potatoes. Or foods such as fish and chicken breasts coated in egg and bread crumbs, then sautéed and served with herb butter and sometimes truffles.

Rillettes (REE-yett). Pork, duck, or other meats cooked in their own fat, pounded or pulverized, then preserved. *Rillettes* are served cool or at room temperature with sliced French bread as an appetizer. (See also Regional/Seasonal Specialties: The Loire.)

Ris de veau (REE deh VOH). Sweetbreads. The thymus gland of young calves. They're quite rich but have a mild, nutty flavor.

Rissolé (REE-so-LAY). Food that has been browned or fried such as *pommes de terre rissolées,* fried potatoes. Also, a sweet turnover. (See Regional/Seasonal Specialties: Franche-Comté, Savoy, and the Dauphiné.)

Riz (ree). Rice.

Robert (ro-BAIR). *Sauce Robert* is an onion sauce with mustard, vinegar, and white wine that is sometimes served with pork or pork chops.

Rognon (ron-YON). Kidney, usually of a lamb or calf. Those who aren't keen on them often compare their aroma to that of, not surprisingly, urine.

Romarin (RO-mah-RAN). Rosemary. This fragrant herb grows well in southern France.

Roquefort (roke-FOR). A blue-veined cheese made from sheep's milk. (See Market Buying Tips and Regional/Seasonal Specialties: Languedoc.)

Roquette (ro-KETT). Rocket lettuce, a salad green. Also known as arugula.

Rosbif (rose-BEEF). Roast beef.

Rôti (ro-TEE). Roasted. *Poulet rôti* (poo-LAY ro-TEE), roasted chicken, is one of the most popular bistro offerings in France.

Rouget (roo-JHAY). Red mullet, an exceptional saltwater fish.

Rouille (roo-EE). Literally, "rust," spicy mayonnaise seasoned with red peppers and garlic, served with fish soups.

Roulade (roo-LAHD). A thin slice of rolled meat or fish, sometimes stuffed.

Roulé (roo-LAY). Rolled. Refers to meats.

Rumsteak (RUM-stake). Rump steak.

(à la) Russe (ah lah ROOSE). Russian-style, e.g., *Salade Russe* (sah-lahd ROOSE), mixed diced vegetables dressed with mayonnaise, and *Charlotte Russe* (shar-LOHT ROOSE), a dessert consisting of a ladyfinger shell filled with a rich, creamy mixture known as Bavarian cream.

Sabayon (sah-bah-YOHN). A frothy blend of egg yolks and wine, served as a sauce or sweetened and served as a dessert or dessert sauce.

Sablé (sah-BLAY). Literally, "sanded," rich, shortbread-type cookies.

Safran (sah-FRAHN). Saffron, a spice used frequently in southern France to flavor breads, rice, soups, and shellfish dishes.

Saignant (sayn-YAHN). Rare, underdone steak, lamb chops, and other meats. Be advised that "rare" in France may be rarer than meats served "rare" in the States.

(à la) Saint-Germain (ah lah sahn-jher-MAHN). In the style of Saint-Germain, a region in the Île de France that was once famous for its peas. *Potage Saint-Germain* (poh-tajh sahn-jher-MAHN) is pea soup.

(gâteau) Saint Honoré (gah-toh SAHN tohn-oh-RAY). A dessert consisting of a custard-filled ring of pastry

topped with cream puffs that have been glazed with caramel icing.

Saint-Pierre (SAHN-pee-AIR). St. Peter fish or John Dory fish. It is called St. Peter fish because of the dark spots on either side of its body, said to suggest St. Peter's thumb marks.

Saison (seh-ZOHN). Season, as in seasonal fruits or vegetables.

Salade (sah-LAHD). Salad. *Salade verte* (sah-LAHD VAIRT) is a green salad made with lettuce, usually a form of cos lettuce. *Salade composée* (sah-LAHD kom-po-ZAY) is a salad with ingredients added (such as meats and cheeses) other than lettuces or a substantial salad that can be served as lunch or a light meal. (See also Comfort Foods: Salad.)

Salmis (sal-MEE). Game or poultry that is roasted until it is half-cooked, then finished in a wine sauce.

Salon (sah-LOHN). Literally, "sitting room." A *salon de thé* (sah-LOHN deh TAY) is a tearoom.

Sauce (soss). Sauce.

Saucisse (soh-SEES). Cooked sausages sliced and served cold as a first course.

Sauge (sohjh). Sage, the herb.

Saumon (so-MAHN). Salmon.

Sauté (so-TAY). Literally, "jumped" or "tossed." Foods (especially meats, poultry, fish, and vegetables) that have been cooked in an uncovered skillet, usually in a little oil or butter, until lightly browned.

Sauvage (so-VAHJH). Wild, uncultivated, as in mushrooms or duck.

Savarin (sah-vah-RAN). A ring-shaped yeast cake soaked in rum or kirsch and filled with a pastry cream.

(à la) Savoyarde (ah lah sa-voy-ARD). In the style of Savoy, dishes prepared with or served with cheese and potatoes. (See Regional/Seasonal Specialties: Franche-Comté, Savoy, and the Dauphiné.)

Sec (sek), and the feminine, *sèche* (sesh). Dry. Often used in reference to certain wines. (See Beverages A to Z.)

Sel (sell). Salt.

Selle (sell). Saddle, as in *selle d'agneau* (sell dan-YOH), saddle of lamb, and *selle de veau* (sell deh VOH), saddle of veal.

Sirop (see-ROP). Syrup.

Socca (SOH-kah). A thin, flat cake of chickpea flour that is a specialty of Nice. (See Regional/Seasonal Specialties: Provence.)

Soubise (soo-BEEZ). A rich, velvety combination of béchamel sauce and puréed onions.

Soupe (soop). Soup. (See Comfort Foods: Soup.)

Spaetzle (shpeht-sehl). Small dumplings made with flour, eggs, and water or milk that are boiled in broth or water, then tossed with butter or added to soups or stews. *Spaetzle* is a German dish that is also enjoyed in Alsace. (See Regional/Seasonal Specialties: Alsace-Lorraine.)

Steak au poivre (stake oh PWAHV). Beefsteak topped with crushed peppercorns, sometimes flamed with brandy and served with a cream sauce.

Steak frites (STAKE fwee). Steak and French fries, a popular combination offered at most bistros.

Steak tartare (stake tahr-TAHR). Minced raw steak served with a raw egg, chopped onions, and capers. For carnivores who feel in need of a little iron boost, this is the ticket.

Sucre (SOO-kruh). Sugar.

Sucré (soo-KRAY). Sweetened, sugared.

Suprême (de volaille) (soo-PREHM deh vo-LI-yee). The breast and wing of chicken or game, also known as *blanc de volaille* (BLAHN deh vo-LI-yee) or *côtelette de volaille* (koh-tell-ETT deh vo-LI-yee).

Table d'hôte (TAH-bluh DOHT). Meal of several courses served at a fixed price.

Tapenade (tah-pe-NAHD).A thick paste made with capers, olives, and olive oil, a specialty of Provence, usually served as a condiment with crudités, fish, and meat.

Tartare (tahr-TAHR). A sauce made with mayonnaise, onions, herbs, capers, and mustard. (See also *Steak tartare.*)

Tarte (tahrt). Tart. An open-faced pie, either sweet or savory.

Tarte flambée (tahrt flahm-BAY). See *Flammekueche.*

Tarte aux noix (TAHR-toh-NWAH). Walnut tart. (See Regional/Seasonal Specialties: Franche-Comté, Savoy, and the Dauphiné.)

Tarte tatin (tahrt tah-TAN). An upside-down apple pie. (See Regional/Seasonal Specialties: The Loire.)

Terrine (teh-REEN). A baking dish in which pâtés are often cooked. The word "terrine" can also refer to the contents of the baking dish itself, usually a meat or vegetable mixture.

Thon (tohn). Tuna.

Thym (tahm). Thyme.

Timbale (tihm-BAHL). A round mold used to bake various dishes. Or food cooked in said round mold.

Tomate (to-MAHT). Tomato. Used prolifically in southern France. (See Regional/Seasonal Specialties: Provence.)

Tournedos (toor-nah-DOH). Small beefsteak cut from the thickest part of the filet.

Touron (too-ROHN). An almond-flavored cake of Spanish origin. (See Regional/Seasonal Specialties: The Pays Basque, Gascony, and the Pyrénées.)

Tourteau fromage (TOOR-toh fro-MAHJH). A kind of cheesecake. It is a specialty of Poitou-Charentes in the Southwest.

Tourtière (TOOR-tee-AIR). A double-crust tart. (See Regional/Seasonal Specialties: The Pays Basque, Gascony, and the Pyrénées.)

Truffe (troof). Truffle, the prized black fungus that grows underground. Truffles are in season in autumn and winter and are quite expensive. A little goes a long way, however. Thin shavings of truffles on top of rice, pasta, or scrambled eggs are all that is needed to flavor the food.

Truffes au chocolat (TROO-foh-SHOH-koh-LAH). Chocolate truffles. Nubby, roundish chocolate candies named after the fungus of the same name (see above) because of the resemblance in shape and color.

Truite (tweet). Trout. One of the best dishes for the dieting traveler is *truite au bleu* (tweet oh bluh), trout that is plunged into boiling water or broth, causing its skin to turn blue in color.

Truite de mer (tweet deh MAIR). Salmon trout.

Ttoro (toh-ro). The local fish stew of the Pays Basque. (See Regional/Seasonal Specialties: The Pays Basque, Gascony, and the Pyrénées.)

Tuile (tweel). Literally, "tile," a thin, curved cookie shaped like a roof tile. These crisp, rather fragile cookies are often served with sorbet or ice cream.

Vanille (va-NEE-yuh). Vanilla.

Vapeur (vah-PURR). Steam, e.g., *pommes (de terre) vapeurs*, steamed potatoes.

Varié (VAH-ree-AY). Assorted. The term can be used to describe a variety of fruits, vegetables, or anything, presented as one serving or on one platter.

Veau (voh). Veal.

Velouté (veh-loo-TAY). Literally, "velvety," a smooth white sauce made with veal, poultry, or fish stock.

Verdure (vehr-DUHR). Green vegetables. Be advised that vegetables served as an accompaniment to chicken, chops, or fish will probably not be a very generous serving. If you want a lot of vegetables, order them à la carte.

Verveine (vair-VEHN). Verbena, a fragrant herb with citruslike hints, often used to make herb tea.

Viande (vee-AHND). Meat.

(à la) Vichyssoise (ah lah vee-chee-SWAHZ). In the style of Vichy, or potato and leek soup.

(à la) Viennoise (ah lah VEE-en-WAHZ). Viennese-style, foods (especially veal) that have been coated in beaten eggs, then in bread crumbs, then fried.

Vinaigre (vee-NEH-gruh). Vinegar.

Vinaigrette (VEE-neh-GRETT). A sauce made with oil and vinegar and sometimes mustard or herbs, the most common dressing for salads in France.

Volaille (vo-LL-yee). Poultry, fowl.

Zewelwai (seh-wel-wah). A quichelike vegetable tart. (See Regional/Seasonal Specialties: Alsace-Lorraine.)

BEVERAGES A TO Z

• ■ •

WILL IT BE BEER, wine, cider, or mineral water? Or how about an apéritif, fresh lemonade, or something to help digest dinner? In France, there's a beverage to go with just about everything, depending on the situation, the food, and the time of day. And, not suprisingly, the French take great pains to make drinks decadent (like melting chocolate bars into hot chocolate), useful (such as making herb teas to cure stomachaches, headaches, and just about every other ailment), and ceremonial (like having fresh lemon juice, a pitcher of water, ice cubes, and sugar brought to the table so that something as simple as making lemonade becomes almost ritualistic).

The French usually begin the day with coffee, tea, or hot chocolate, which are available at any hotel restaurant or café. If you go to a café, you are likely to see a mix of blue-collar workers downing tiny cups of black espresso, college students studying over big cups of *café au lait*, and suited professionals of both sexes sipping anything caffeinated. This morning ritual crosses all socioeconomic boundaries, and the traveler can witness a real slice of life by watching the morning café activity. (Of course, the clientele will depend on the café's location. If it's near the Louvre, it may be full of tourists! To be a part of the French "scene," wander off the beaten path a bit.)

. A description of the most popular morning beverages follows:

COFFEE

Café (kah-FAY). Coffee. (The word also refers to the type of restaurant that serves coffee and simple foods.) *Un café* (ahn kah-FAY), or a cup of coffee, refers to a small cup (about two to three ounces) of strong, black espresso. Sugar will be served alongside your *café*, but milk and cream will not. *Café* packs a punch, so if you need an eye-opener, this is the trick. (It is also referred to as *café express;* see below.) In fancy establishments, *café* is often served with individually wrapped pieces of bittersweet chocolate.

Café décaféiné (kah-FAY day-kah-fay-ee-NAY) or, *café déca* (kah-FAY DAY-kah). Decaffeinated coffee.

Café express (kah-FAY eks-PRESS). Espresso; dark, black strong coffee served in small cups. It is consumed black, with sugar if desired.

Café filtre (kah-FAY FIL-truh). American-style coffee, made by pouring boiling water over fresh coffee grounds in a filter. *Café filtre* is usually somewhat stronger and darker than typical American coffee.

Café au lait (kah-FAY oh lay) or *Café crème* (kah-FAY krem). Strong, dark coffee mixed with warm or steamed milk. (Note to calorie watchers: The milk used here is usually full-fat whole milk. If you want low-fat milk—*lait écrémé* (lay TAY-kreh-may)—your request will probably not be granted unless you are in a large, tourist-driven *café*. The French do not consume much milk as a beverage, so most eating establishments do not carry different kinds of milk.
Note: The French never drink coffee *before* a meal or *with* a meal except breakfast. Sometimes espresso is sipped *with* dessert after lunch or dinner, but usually it is served *after* dessert, as a course all its own.

TEA

Thé (tay), *thé au lait* (TAY oh LAY), *thé citron* (tay SEE-trohn). Tea, tea with milk, and tea with lemon. *Tisane* (tee-ZAHN) is herb tea, an infusion of various edible herbs or flowers steeped in boiling water. Most tisanes are purported to have some medicinal properties, for instance, aiding digestion and inducing sleep.

At a basic café, your tea will probably be served in a small pot filled with hot water and a tea bag or two. At a fancier café or *salon de thé* (sah-LOHN deh TAY), a tearoom, there will be much pomp and circumstance when your tea is served. You will probably be able to choose the type of tea you want (such as Darjeeling, Earl Grey, and oolong), which will be brewed (loose leaves, not tea bags), then strained through a silver or porcelain strainer. Whether you opt for milk or lemon, you will be offered sugar to add if you like and, possibly, some bittersweet chocolates for munching.

CHOCOLATE

Chocolat chaud (SHOH-koh LAH shoh). Hot chocolate. In fancy restaurants and tearooms, hot chocolate can be as rich as dessert, as it is sometimes made with melted chocolate bars and topped with whipped cream—*chantilly* (SHAN-tee-yee).

WATER

Eau (singular) and *eaux* (plural) are both pronounced the same, oh.

The drinking of bottled water began at a time when, in some parts of the world, available water—such as that out of the tap—was questionable. Now, even though in most of France tap water is drinkable, there is still a big tradition of drinking bottled water. It has even become status-driven: Some waters are considered more chic than others. Water terminology is as follows:

Eau gazeuse (oh gah-ZOOHZ). Fizzy or sparkling mineral water.

Eau minérale (oh ME-neh rahl). Mineral water. This term usually refers to nonsparkling water.

CIDER

Cidre (SEE-druh). Apple or pear cider. A specialty of Brittany and Normandy, *cidre* is slightly alcoholic and not as sweet as most American apple ciders, which are basically fresh-pressed apples. Cold and tangy-sweet cider is delicious all on its own, sipped from mugs on a warm summer afternoon or as an accompaniment to picnic fare or rustic country dishes. (See also Regional/Seasonal Specialties: Normandy.)

Cidre bouché (SEE-druh boo-shay). Sparkling cider that is about 6 percent alcohol.

Cidre brut (SEE-druh broot). Cider that is about 4 percent alcohol.

Cidre doux (SEE-druh doo). Cider that is about 2 percent alcohol.

JUICE/CITRUS

Citron pressé (sih-TROHN preh-SAY). Lemonade, usually served as fresh lemon juice over ice accompanied by sugar and water, to be added as desired.

Jus d'orange (jhoo do-RAHNJH). Orange juice.

BEER

Bière (bee-YAIR). Beer can be pale, *blonde* (blond); brown ale, *brune* (broon); or *pression* (PRE-see-YON) draft. Bottled beer is *bière bouteille* (bee-YAIR boo-tay). For a refreshing, lower-in-alcohol beverage, ask for a shandy, a *bière limonade* (bee-YAIR lee-moh-NAHD).

The traveler will find beer at all cafés, bars, and restaurants, but the biggest selection is likely to be at a casual restaurant known as a brasserie (BRAH-suh-REE).

APÉRITIF

The word *apéritif* literally means "appetizing." Apéritifs are a family of drinks that were originally sipped before lunch or dinner to stimulate the appetite. Few of us need appetite stimulants these days, but apéritifs are alive and well and a good (read: lower in alcohol) alternative to American-style cocktails. Some of the most popular apéritifs are *kir* (keer), vermouth, and *anis* (ah-NEES) and *pastis* (pah-STEES); the last two are licorice-flavored drinks served with ice and a pitcher of water to mix as desired. Various brands include Pernod and Ricard. These pale yellow, cloudy liquids are usually mixed with water and served on the rocks. Kir is an apéritif of dry white wine and *crème de cassis*, which is a specialty of Burgundy. Other favorite apéritifs include *Dubonnet* (DOO-boh-NAY), a pleasant, bittersweet wine-based drink usually served on the rocks with a lemon twist. The French also enjoy Italian apéritifs such as *Campari* (kahm-PAR-ee).

Many bars and restaurants feature an *apéritif maison* (ah-PAY-ruh TEEF may-ZON), or "house drink," which is the establishment's own creation and often a champagne-based drink. A simple glass of champagne may also be considered an apéritif, as are champagne-based drinks such as *kir royale* (KEER roy-AL), a specialty of Dijon and the Burgundy region made with champagne or sparkling wine and *crème de cassis* (KREHM deh kah-SEES). Another popular champagne drink combines champagne plus *crème de framboise* (KREHM deh frahm-BWAHZ), raspberry liqueur. If you simply must have "the usual," most bars and restaurants offer basic spirits—bourbon, scotch, vodka, gin—but only big, tourist-driven restaurants or hotel bars are likely to make fancy cocktails. Instead, opt for simple mixers, like orange juice (*jus d'orange*, jhoo do-RAHNJH), tonic water (called *eau tonique*, oh tohn-EEK, Indian or Indian tonic in France).

And, of course, it is perfectly acceptable to have a nonalcoholic drink before dinner. Mineral water, tonic water, and orange juice are good choices that won't spoil your appetite.

AFTER-DINNER DRINKS

A *digestif* (DEE-jes-TEEF) is a term that includes spirits served after dinner, such as brandy, eaux-de-vie, and liqueurs. The word "digestif" is a bit misleading because while strong spirits may *seem* like a digestive aid, they may actually make your stomach feel worse the next day if you've already had an apéritif and several glasses of wine. A listing of some of the more popular after-dinner drinks follows:

Armagnac (AR-mahn-YAK). A type of brandy, similar to cognac, that is made in the town of Armagnac in southwestern France.

Calvados (KAL-vah-DOHS). A strong brandy made from apples in the town of Calvados in Normandy.

Chartreuse (shar-TRUHZ). A fragrant liqueur that is made in two versions: green and yellow (the flavors are slightly different). Both have a mildly bitter, very herbaceous taste. If you like Campari, you will probably like Chartreuse.

Cognac (KOHN-yak). A brandy from the town of the same name, this is considered the best of all brandies. The stars on the label indicate the cognac's age: One star means aged at least three years; two stars, four years; and three stars means the cognac has aged at least five years. When a cognac has aged longer than five years, it is labeled V.S. (Very Superior), V.S.O.P. (Very Superior Old Pale), or V.V.S.O.P. (Very Very Superior Old Pale).

Eaux-de-vie (OH dch-VEE). Very strong, colorless spirits distilled from fruit juice.

Kirsch (keersch). Colorless, distilled spirits made from cherries and their pits. Kirsch is an eau-de-vie and is made in Alsace.

Mirabelle (mee-ruh-BEHL). Eau-de-vie made from plums.

WINE

Lunch and dinner in France—no matter how simple—are nearly always enjoyed with wine. This custom crosses all socioeconomic boundaries; wine is everyman's drink, appreciated by rich, poor, young, old, and in-between. Children are sometimes introduced to wine at a young age and on special occasions are given a little taste of wine that has been diluted with water. And, by age fourteen, a French boy or girl can be served wine in a restaurant. Because they grow up drinking it, wine is not thought of as something complicated or intimidating. The French take wine drinking seriously (it is, after all, an integral part of the meal), but they do not necessarily know every detail about every wine. The average Frenchman or woman *does*, however, seem to have an innate knowledge about wine, but it's not necessarily because he or she has been taking classes or reading books; wine is simply a part of his or her heritage, part of dining, part of life. While very expensive, luxury wines are typically enjoyed by those with deep pockets, even these wines are not considered mysterious or unapproachable; they are simply considered special-occasion beverages, to be consumed with respect but above all to be enjoyed.

Since wine is such an important part of their lives, it is not surprising to discover that the French produce about one fourth of the world's total and, as a group, *consume* more wine per capita than any other country. And although alcoholism and liver disease are indeed problems in France, public drunkenness is fairly uncommon and considered unacceptable. Wine is generally served *with* meals, not before (except perhaps a glass of dry white wine or champagne as an apéritif). When consumed with food, the alcohol in the wine is absorbed into the system more slowly, so overdoing it is less likely. But if in your enthusiasm for French wine and food you find you have imbibed too much, go to the pharmacy (usually designated by a sign with a green cross), point to your head and/or your stomach, and tell the pharmacist you have a hangover—a *gueule de bois* (GOOL-deh-BWAH). The French have all kinds of over-the-counter elixirs, pills, and herbal teas for setting your system straight again. Many of these "cures" contain fennel, mint, or other medicinal herbs that should help settle your tummy.

There is definitely an allure about French wines, which has led to an undeserved reputation that they are expensive. True, the top wines from Burgundy and Bordeaux can be costly. But there are many, many inexpensive wines made in France, and the informed traveler will find many very affordable choices. Remember, you'll be avoiding import taxes, so that bottle of Chablis purchased in a French wineshop might cost twice as much back home in the States.

This section is designed to help the traveler understand wine by including the following:

1. A vocabulary of wine basics.
2. Terms for appreciating wine.
3. How to order wine in a restaurant.
4. A summary of the main wine regions of France.

Armed with the above information, the traveler should be able to order wine in a restaurant and choose wines in a wineshop with reasonable confidence. And don't forget: You're allowed to bring back two bottles duty-free into the U.S.A. It's a good idea to take a few yards of bubble pack with you to protect wines you're bringing home. Lacking bubble pack, you can stuff bottles into several thicknesses of hiking socks. (And if you aren't buying wine, you can use the bubble pack to wrap jars of olives, honey, walnut oil, and raspberry vinegar.)

Wine Basics

A.O.C. These initials stand for *Appellation d'Origine Contrôlée* (AH-peh-LAH-see-ON DO-ree-jheen KOHN-tro-lay) and refer to the laws that control wine production in France. According to French law, there are four levels of wine:

1. *Appellation Contrôlée* (AH-peh-LAH-see-ON KOHN-tro-lay), also noted on the label as A.O.C. or A.C. This is the top level of wine, the highest rank.
2. *Vin Délimité de Qualité Supérieure* (VAN day-lee-mee-TAY deh KAH-lee-TAY SOO-pee-ree-YUR), the second level of quality, also noted on the label as V.D.Q.S.
3. *Vin de Pays* (VAN deh pay-EES). Literally, "country wine," just below VDQS in terms of quality.
4. *Vin de table* (VAN deh TAH-bluh). Ordinary table wines. Just below *Vin de pays* in terms of quality.

Wine Terms

Crémant (kray-MAHN). Literally, "creaming," wines that are slightly effervescent but not as bubbly as champagne.

Cru (kroo). This term refers to growth or to a vineyard.

Cru Bourgeois (KROO boo-JHWAZ). Wines just below *Grand Cru Classé*. (Don't let the term *bourgeois* throw you; there are some excellent wines in this category.)

Cru Classé (KROO klah-SAY). Literally, "classed growth." The term refers to a Château—usually in Bordeaux—that is in the top ranks.

Cuvée (koo-VAY). Vintage; contents of the vat. In Champagne, the word refers to a batch of blended wines. Outside Champagne, *cuvée* may refer to a blend of wines from different vineyards, or a blend of different varieties.

Deuxième Cru (DEU-zyehm KROO). Literally, "second growth," the second highest subcategory of the *cru* classes wines of the Médoc and Sauternes.

Grand Cru (grahn KROO). A vineyard designated as a "great growth." In Burgundy, *Grand Cru* is the highest ranking a vineyard can receive. Generally speaking, a *Grand Cru* wine is one that comes from a very good vineyard, a level above *Premier Cru*.

Grand Cru Classé (grahn KROO klah-SAY). The second highest category for wines in Bordeaux.

Premier Cru (preh-myay KROO). "First growth." In the regions of Médoc and Sauternes, *Premier Cru* is the highest subcategory of *Cru Classé*.

Premier Grand Cru (preh-MYAY grahn KROO). "First great growth."

Premier Grand Cru Classé (preh-MYAY grahn KROO klah-SAY). "First great classed growth," the highest category for wines of the Saint-Émilion region of Bordeaux. Also, "first-growth" wines of the Médoc and Sauternes may use *Premier Grand Cru Classé* on their labels.

Terms for Appreciating Wine

Bouquet. The fragrance, or aroma, of the wine.

Breathe. Certain wines are allowed to "breathe," or aerate, as exposure to air can rid the wine of "off" odors. Breathing can also help bring out the wine's bouquet.

Carafe (Kah-RAFF). A decanter or glass bottle for serving wines.

Decanting. Pouring the wine from one container to another to aerate the wine and eliminate sediment.

Legs. Trails of liquid on the inside of a wine glass that indicate high levels of glycerin and alcohol.

Nonvintage. A wine made from a blend of grapes from two or more years. Also called NV.

Nose. In winespeak, "nose " is used to refer to the wine's aroma and bouquet.

Perfume. Fragrant, floral smells in the nose of some wines.

Vintage. The term that describes the year of the harvest and, therefore, the wine made from those grapes.

Ordering Wine in a Restaurant

In France, fancy restaurants will have a wine steward—*sommelier* (soh-mahl-YAY) or *sommelière* (soh-malh-LYAIR) if female—who can help with the wine order. Wine service in such establishments is taken seriously, but the *sommelier's* job is not to intimidate but to help choose the best wine within your budget to go with the food you have ordered. If you have no budget, let the *sommelier* choose for you; he frequently will come up with something you might not have considered, and you will generally be pleased.

Here's the routine: The *sommelier* (or, in simpler

restaurants, the waiter) will hand you a wine list, the *carte des vins*. Take your time to peruse the list, and refer to pocket-sized vintage charts (available free from some wineshops in the States) if you need to. Tell the *sommelier* what you want—or simply point to it. The waiter will take the wine list and return with the wine. He will then present the wine to you.

Look at the label to make sure it is the wine you ordered, taking particular care to check the vintage date. (The difference between a 1985 and a 1984, for example, can be massive, both in terms of the wine quality and the price.) Say *"oui"* (wee) or nod "yes" if it is the correct wine. The *sommelier* will open the wine, then present you with the cork. Traditionally, the cork was to be sniffed to detect any "off" odors. Most wine drinkers rarely sniff the cork, but if you want to, go ahead and sniff. It's a good idea, however, to *look* at the cork to see if it is crumbly or moldy, which may indicate that the wine was not stored or handled properly, which might therefore affect its quality. Place the cork on the table and nod "yes." The *sommelier* will pour you a little wine to taste. Swirl it (to aerate it slightly), sniff it, and take a sip. Unless the wine has a vinegary, moldy, or other unpleasant odor or taste, it is probably fine. At that point, nod "yes" to the *sommelier* so that he can then pour wine for others at the table and give you some more.

Note: If you taste a wine and decide you simply don't like it, you will have a difficult time sending it back. The practice of sending wines back is only for bottles that are truly "off," that is, they have been stored or corked improperly and taste bad. If you think the wine might be "off," ask the *sommelier* to taste it; most of them are honest (although many can be chauvinistic) and will take a bottle back if it is truly bad.

The Major Wine-Producing Regions
Bordeaux

Bordeaux is a region located in southwestern France. It produces 10 percent of all French wines, most of which are reds, but a small percentage of which are dry whites. Only 2 percent of all Bordeaux are sweet whites. In Bordeaux, the most famous wine districts are Médoc, Graves, Saint-Émilion, Pomerol, and Sauternes. Here is a brief description of each district:

1. *Médoc* (may-DOK). The Médoc is divided into two subdistricts: Médoc and *Haut-Médoc* (oh-may-DOK). The Haut-Médoc includes four communes: *Saint Estèphe* (SAHN eh-steff), *Pauillac* (POH-yak), *Saint Julien* (SAHN jhoo-lee-EHN), and *Margaux* (mar-GOH). The Médoc is Bordeaux's largest and best-known wine region. The main red grapes used in the Médoc are cabernet franc, cabernet sauvignon, and merlot plus some petit verdot and malbec.

2. *Graves* (grahv). Graves produces mostly white wine made from sauvignon blanc and *Sémillion* (seh-mee-YOHN) grapes. Top-notch dry white Graves wines are bright, clean, and lively when young and rich, robust and full-bodied when they've aged.

3. *Saint-Émilion* (SAHN eh-mee-YOHN). The sec-

ond most important wine-making district in Bordeaux.

4. *Pomerol* (POH-me-rohl). The smallest of the fine-wine producing districts of Bordeaux.

5. *Sauternes* (saw-TURN). Produces sweet white wines made primarily from the Sémillion grape.

Burgundy

Burgundy is located in central-eastern France and is as important as Bordeaux in terms of the first-rate wines it produces. Burgundy, however, produces about 75 percent less wine by volume, which is why great Burgundies are usually expensive. They are, quite simply, very scarce. Most of the wine made in Burgundy is red, but there are well-known whites, too, especially those made in Chablis (which makes nothing but whites) and the Mâconnais.

There are five major wine districts in Burgundy: Chablis, Côte d'Or, Côte Chalonnaise, Mâconnais, and Beaujolais. Descriptions and summaries of each follow

1. *Chablis* (sha-BLEE). Wines in this region are all white and made from the chardonnay grape. Because of the climate and soil in this region, Chablis wines tend to be more austere than other white Burgundies. True Chablis are very dry, clean, crisp, and bracing. They have lively acidity, which makes them a good match for oysters and other shellfish. (Think of what a squeeze of lemon does for shellfish; the natural acidity in Chablis com-

plements shellfish in a similar fashion.) Chablis are classified as follows, from the simplest to the best:

- *Petit Chablis* (peh-TEE sha-BLEE)
- *Chablis* (sha-BLEE)
- *Chablis Première* Cru (sha-BLEE preh-mee-YAIR KROO)
- *Chablis Grand Cru* (sha-BLEE grahn KROO).

2. The *Côte d'Or* (koht DOHR) is divided into the *Côte de Nuits* (KOHT deh NWEE), which produces red wines, and the *Côte de Beaune* (KOHT deh BONE), which produces reds and whites. Côte d'Or wines are classified as follows, from the simplest to the grandest:

- *Village* (vee-AJH)
- *Première Cru* (preh-mee-YAIR KROO)
- *Grand Cru* (grahn KROO)

3. *Côte Chalonnaise* (KOHT sha-loh-NAYZ). The most important areas in this district are *Givry* (jhih-VREE) and *Mercurey* (mehr-kyer-AY), both of which produce mostly red wines from the pinot noir grape; *Montagny* (mohn-tahn-YEE), which produces only white wines (from the chardonnay grape); and *Rully* (roo-YEE), which produces equal amounts of reds (from pinot noir grapes) and whites (from chardonnay grapes).

4. *Mâconnais* (MAH-koh-NAY). Wines from the Mâconnais are mostly white and made from the chardonnay grape. Wines in the region are classi-

fied as follows, from the simplest to the finest: *Mâcon Blanc* (MAH-kohn BLAHN), *Mâcon Supérieur* (MAH-kohn soo-PEH-ree-UR), and *Mâcon Villages* (MAH-kohn vee-YAJH). At the top of the heap are several individual villages with their own appellations. They include *Pouilly Fuissé* (poo-YEE foo-SAY), *Pouilly Loché* (poo-YEE lo-SHAY), *Pouilly Vinzelles* (poo-YEE van-ZELL), and *Saint Véran* (SAHN veh-RAHN).

5. *Beaujolais* (BO-jho-LAY). The lively reds made in this region are made from 100 percent gamay grapes. Beaujolais are typically light and fruity and meant to be drunk young. The wines in Beaujolais are classified as follows:

- *Beaujolais*. Basic Beaujolais.
- *Beaujolais Supérieur* (BO-jho-LAY soo-PEH-ree-UR). Basic *Beaujolais* with a higher alcohol content.
- *Beaujolais-Villages*. *Beaujolais* wine from specific villages in Beaujolais. Most *Beaujolais-Villages* are made from a blend of wines from the villages.
- *Beaujolais Nouveau* (BO-jho-LAY noo-VO). Wine that is released the third Thursday in November that is the current year's harvest. (Made with grapes picked and crushed only a few weeks earlier. It is very light and fruity and meant to be consumed within a few months.)
- *Beaujolais-Cru*. There are ten *cru* (villages) that produce the best *Beaujolais*:
  Brouilly (broo-YEE)
  Chénas (SHAY-nahs)

Chiroubles (shee-ROO-bluh)
Côte de Brouilly (KOTE deh broo-YEE)
Fleurie (flu-REE)
Juliénas (JHOO-lee-AIN-ahs)
Morgon (mor-GON)
Moulin-à-Vent (moo-LAHN-ah-VAHN)
Régénie (RAY-jhe-NEE)
Saint-Amour (SAHN-tah-MOOR)

Note: Wines from the above *crus* do not usually have the word *Beaujolais* on the label.

The Loire Valley

This region in northwestern France makes some red and rosé wines, but it is most famous for its whites. The best known are the wines from *Sancerre* (sahn-SEHR) and *Pouilly Fumé* (Poo-YEE foo-MAY), two fresh, crisp whites made from the sauvignon blanc grape. Another white wine grape that flourishes in the Loire Valley is the chenin blanc, which makes another famous Loire white: *Vouvray* (voo-VRAY), named after an area near Tours; *Vouvray* wines are vinified (turned into wine) in three different styles: dry, medium-dry, and sweet. There are even some sparkling Vouvrays, made in the same method as champagne.

Another famous white wine from the Loire is *muscadet* (mcuh-skah DAY), which is made from a white grape called *melon de Bourgogne* (meh-LONN-deh boor-GOHN yuh). The three levels of *muscadet* are as follows:

- *Muscadet AC*
- *Muscadet Sèvre-et-Maine*
- *Muscadet des Côteaux de la Loire AC*

Muscadets are usually light, very dry, and a good accompaniment to clams, oysters, and fish. They are best consumed young.

One of the finest *rosés* in France is made in the Loire in a town called Anjou. Look for *Rosé d'Anjou* (RO-zay dahn-JHOO) when you want something light and fruity to enjoy with cold poached chicken, salmon, or other picnic fare. As for true red wines, the best in the Loire come from Touraine. They are *Chinon* (she-NOHN) and *Bourgueil* (boor-GEUH-yuh), both made from a blend of cabernet sauvignon and cabernet franc grapes. They are typically light and fruity.

Alsace

Alsatian wines are often confused with German wines because both are made with the same grape varieties: *pinot blanc* (PEE-noh BLAHN), *pinot gris* (PEE-noh GREE), *Riesling* (REE-sleeng), and *Gewürztztraminer* (guh-WURTZ-trah-mee-ner). The difference in Alsatian and German wines is that Alsatian wines tend to be drier and higher in alcohol.

There is a small amount of red wine made in Alsace, but over 90 percent of it is white. Perhaps the best-known Alsatian white is Riesling, which has a floral bouquet but is crisp and dry in the mouth. Alsatian Riesling is good with fish, shellfish, poultry, and as an apéritif. *Gewürtztraminer* (the word in German means "spicy") also has a slightly floral nose but is lower in acidity than Riesling, so it tends to be rather soft and supple in the mouth. It is good paired up with rich cheeses and foie gras as well as *choucroute garnie*, smoked foods, and Munster cheese. Alsatian wines made from the pinot gris grape—also known as *Tokay pinot gris* (toh-KAY PEE-noh GREE) or *Tokay d'Alsace* (toh-KAY dahl-SAHS)—is rich and full-bodied, a good choice with game birds or roast chicken.

Alsatian Wine Terms

Vendage Tardive (van-dajh tar-DEEV). A term that literally means "late harvest." It refers to Alsatian wines that are rich, flavorful, and totally dry.

Sélection de Grains Nobles (seh-LEK-see-OHN deh GRAHN NOH-bluh). A term used to describe Alsatian wines made with late-harvest grapes that have been affected with a mold, which results in a sweet, concentrated wine. (Note: This is the same mold that creates the sweet white Bordeaux wine *sauternes*.)

Champagne

Ahhhhhh, Champagne. This sparkly drink denotes good times and special occasions. It is made in an area of northern France of the same name, and it is *only* made in this region. "Champagne" cannot be made in California, or Spain, or Italy. Countries other than France produce very good effervescent wines, indeed, but champagne is made only in Champagne; there is no such thing as "California champagne."

True Champagne is made from one, two, or a blend of three different grapes: chardonnay, *pinot meunier* (PEE-noh muh-NYAY), and pinot noir. When champagne is made from 100 percent chardonnay, the bottle is labeled *Blanc de Blancs* (BLAHN deh BLAHN). Champagne made from 100 percent pinot noir is labeled *Blanc de Noir* (BLAHN deh NWAR). There are also champagnes made with a blend of the two red grapes pinot noir and pinot meunier.

All true champagnes are made by a technique called *Méthode Champenoise* (meh-TOAD SHAM-pee-NWAZ). The process is as follows:

Various still wines that are made in the Champagne region from the grapes mentioned above are blended according to the wine maker's direction. Then a *dosage* (doe-SAJH), a syrupy mixture of wine and dissolved sugar is added along with yeasts, which cause the mixture to ferment. It is then bottled and corked, and the mixture goes through what is known as secondary fermentation. (The first fermentation takes place when the still wine is made from grape juice.) This secondary fermentation produces alcohol and carbon dioxide, which create bubbles in the liquid. The bottles are stored at an angle (bottom end up) for a period of time determined by the wine maker. The bottles are then disgorged. When bottles are disgorged (a process that releases sediment that has settled near the top of the bottle), they are filled with some of the same *cuvée* (the blend of still wines need to make the champagne) to replace the volume lost in disgorgement. The champagne is then tightly capped with the characteristic cork, foil, and wire twist.

Champagne Terms

Brut (broo). Extra dry.

Crémant (KRAY-mahn). Literally means "creaming," but when referring to sparkling wines it refers to wines that are moderately effervescent.

Demi-sec (deh-MEE sek). Champagne that is partially sweet.

Doux (doo). Sweet champagne.

Extra brut (EKS-trah BROO). Even drier than brut.

Sec (SEK). Champagne that is partially dry.

Other Wine-Producing Regions
Rhône Valley

The Rhône valley is located in southeastern France. It is divided into two districts: North and South. Most Rhône wines come from the southern part of the region. Appellations (wine-producing areas) of the south include:

1. *Côte du Rhône* (KOHT du RONE). About 80 percent of wines made in the Rhône come from this

area. Most are reds, but there are a few whites and rosés.

2. *Côtes du Ventoux* (KOTE du vahn-TOO).
3. *Côtes du Rhône-Villages* (KOTE du RONE VEE-yahjh).
4. *Gigondas* (JHEE-gohn-DAHS).
5. *Vaqueyras* (VAH-keh-RAHS).

Two rosés made in the southern Rhône are *Tavel* (tah-VEHL) and *Lirac* (lee-RAHK), which are made mainly from grenache and cinsault grapes.

Châteauneuf-du-Pape (SHAH-toh-nuf du PAHP). Perhaps the best-known wine of the southern Rhône. Most of them are made from grenache, mourvèdre, and syrah grapes.

Northern Rhône

The best-known reds from the northern part of the Rhône valley are also probably the best known in the entire Rhône region: *Côte Rôtie* (KOTE ro-TEE) and *Hermitage* (AIR-mee-TAJH). Both are made from the syrah grape.

As for Northern Rhône whites, there is a small amount of white *Hermitage* made from the Marsanne and Rousanne varieties. The other Northern Rhône white is *Condrieu* (KOHN-dree-YUH), which is made from the *viognier* grape.

COMFORT FOODS
· ■ ·

No matter where you venture, no matter how extraordinary the food, traveling can be exhausting and even the best vacation can leave you longing for something soothing, something familiar. There's a lot to be said for the philosophy "When in Rome, do as the Romans do," as it allows the traveler to experience more fully a foreign place, but even the most ambitious travelers get cravings for things like peanut butter, corn flakes, and diet cola, even in places—like France—where the food is excellent. Generally speaking, we are comforted by foods we grew up with, foods that Mom used to make or foods that we know make us feel better when we're not at our physical best.

Here is a listing of foods that can help quell homesick feelings—eggs and toast, ham and cheese, bread and chocolate, for example—plus foods to know about should you not be feeling well.

Bread. *Pain* (pan). Bread lovers will have a feast in France, a country that prides itself on its vast assortment of baked goods. In terms of variety, French breads run the gamut from the light and elegant to the dense and rustic. If you're longing for simple, sandwich-type bread, ask for *pain de mie* (PAN deh MEE). For whole-wheat bread, look for *pain complet* (PAN kohm-PLEH). The classic French loaf, however, is the *baguette* (ba-GETT), a long, thin "wand" with a crackly crust and a chewy, soft, white interior. A *batârd* (BAH-tahr) is shorter and wider than a *baguette* but tastes much like it. Specialty breads include *pain aux noix* (PAN oh NWAH), walnut bread, often served with the cheese course, and *pain aux olives* (PAN oh zoh-LEEV), olive bread, which can be found throughout the country but particularly in southern France. Want something sweet and rich? Ask for *pain au chocolat* (PAN oh SHOH-koh-LAH), which consists of buttery croissant dough wrapped around a chocolate bar. When it's warm from the baker's oven, the chocolate melts slightly; what a treat! It's sure to soothe a cranky child or an out-of-sorts adult.

Chicken. *Poulet* (poo-LAY). When the traveler has tired of fancy sauces and unfamiliar fare, plain, roast chicken—moist on the inside, golden brown on the outside—can be most welcome. And happily, when it comes to cooking, the French understand simplicity as well as elaboration. Ask for *poulet rôti* (POO-lay roh-TEE), roast chicken, at any bistro, brasserie, or restaurant, and you'll likely get half of a young bird, roasted to perfection, served with French fries.

Cheese. *Fromage* (fro-MAJH). France is perhaps as famous for its cheeses as for its fashions. There are literally hundreds of cheeses, ranging from barely aged types that are soft, mild, and spreadable—like *fromage blanc* (fro-MAJH blah)—to strong, crumbly, blue-veined cheeses that are decidedly not for timid eaters. (See *Fromageries* in Market Buying Tips for descriptions of some of the most popular cheeses in France. Also see Regional/Seasonal Foods for cheeses that are a specialty of the various regions.)

Chocolate. *Chocolat* (SHOH-koh-LAH). One of the easiest cravings to satisfy in France is the one for chocolate. In fact, many of the large cities have shops called *chocolateries* (SHO-koh-LAH-teh-ree) that sell only that: chocolate bars, candies in every imaginable form, some plain and some elaborately filled. You can also find chocolates at candy shops—*confiseries* (kohn-FEE-suh-REE)—throughout France. For a cup of hot chocolate, go to a *salon de thé* (sah-LOHN deh TAY) and ask for a *chocolat chaud* (SHOH-koh-LAH shoh).

- *chocolat amer* (shoh-koh-LAH tah-MAIR). Bittersweet chocolate.
- *chocolat au lait* (SHOH-koh-LAH toh LAY). Milk chocolate.
- *chocolat mi-amer* (shoh-koh-LAH MEE-ah-MAIR). A sweeter version of bittersweet chocolate than *chocolat amer*.

Consommé. *Consommé* (KOHN suh-may). This clear broth, which can be made from beef, game, or poultry, is the cure for just about everything, from a hangover to a cold to an upset tummy.

Cookies. *Biscuits* (bee-SKWEE). It's unlikely that you'll find chocolate chip or oatmeal cookies better than those at home, but savvy shoppers in France will discover deliciously satisfying alternatives. Go to the *pâtisserie* (PAH-tee-suh-REE), or bakery, to find *sablés* (sah-BLAY), or sugar cookies; *macaron* (MAH-ka-ROHN), macaroons; or *financier* (FEE-nahn-see-AY), a rich, buttery almond-flavored confection. And there are *palmiers* (PAHL-mee-AY), sugar- glazed, palm-leaved-shaped sweets made from puff pastry dough. At fancy restaurants and tearooms, the diner may also find refined little confections drizzled with icing, studded with currants, or enriched with pistachios served with after-dinner coffee or tea. Very good packaged cookies can be purchased at grocery stores.

Custard. Called *flan* (flahn), *crème caramel* (KREHM ka-ra-MEHL), *crème renversée* (KREHM rahn-vair-SAY). This simple, easy-to-eat classic dessert is available at most bistros and brasseries throughout France. Made with whole milk or cream, eggs, and sugar, it tastes like your—or someone's—grandmother has been in the kitchen. Note: The word "flan" can also refer to a pastry tart; ask before ordering.

Egg. *Oeuf* (uhf). French cooks work wonders with eggs, and in many cafés you can order an omelette almost any time of day. They are sometimes served with a saucelike *pipérade* (pee-pah-RAHD) or *aurore* (ah-ROAR) as an entrée. As a comfort food, *omelette aux fines herbes*, a green salad, and some French bread can hit the spot for a simple supper or lunch.

Eggs aren't eaten for breakfast in France as much as in the U.S.A., but many hotel restaurants offer them. Usually, you'll see them as *oeuf à la coque* (UHF ah lah KOK), soft-cooked eggs, or as *oeufs durs* (uh DUHR), hard-boiled eggs, which will be served in an egg cup with the shell on. (Take your knife or spoon and tap the shell to crack it, then eat the egg with the spoon.) *Oeufs mollets* (uh moh-YAY) are eggs simmered for six minutes; *oeufs pochés* (uh po-SHAY) are poached eggs. For fried eggs, ask for *oeufs frites* (uh fwee) or *oeuf sauté à la poêle* (uhf sah-TAY ah lah PWAHL). Eggs may also be available in cafés and bistros *sur la plat* (suhr lah PLAH), that is, served in the dish or pan in which they are cooked. Scrambled eggs, *oeufs brouillés* (uh broo-YAY), are not traditionally on most breakfast menus, but some hotels may prepare them upon request.

French fries. *Pommes frites* (pohm FREET). Fries are often served as a side dish to simple bistro fare, like roast chicken or grilled steak. Fries in France are usually slender—but not as as thin as matchsticks—and are very, very good. But don't look for ketchup as an accompaniment; the French eat their fries sprinkled with a little salt, and that's it. Touristy eateries and big hotel restaurants, however, may bring you ketchup (it's the same word in French) upon request. And, by the way, you can eat fries with your fingers, just like back home. With a big plate of fries on the table, most homesick travelers in France won't miss American fast food one bit. (See also Potatoes.)

Ham and cheese sandwich. *Sandwich jambon et fromage* (sand-WEECH jham-BOHN ay froh-MAJH). You'll find sandwiches at nearly every café, but they're a little different from American-style, Dagwood-type sandwiches. French sandwiches are usually served on a sliced *baguette* or other similar crusty loaf rather than sliced American-style bread. The bread will likely be spread with sweet butter—not mayonnaise—and perhaps a little mustard. A French ham and cheese sandwich will usually be made with a mildly smoked, brine-cured ham (much like American sandwich-type ham) and French (not Swiss) *Gruyère* or *Emmental* cheese. And, unlike American sandwiches, which have more filling than bread, French sandwiches are generally the reverse, consisting of thick slabs of crusty bread enclosing a very thin—but very good—filling. Craving a grilled ham and cheese? Ask for a *croque-monsieur* (KROHK-muh-SYUR), which is usually made with the same kinds of ham and cheese as listed above, but for a *croque-monsieur*, they are layered on sliced bread called *pain de mie*.

Hamburger. *Hamburger*. Available at McDonald's (yes, the golden arches exist in France) and other fast-food chains throughout the country. These Gallic renditions of an American classic may satisfy a craving, but don't expect the same flavors and textures that you get from the burgers back home; it seems the French version is made with a different grade of beef than its American cousins.

Ice cream. *Glace* (glahs). The French love ice cream, and it appears on menus everywhere. There are fewer mixed flavors (don't look for things like chunky banana brownie or coconut-peach pecan), but excellent chocolate, vanilla, and coffee ice creams are often served with sauces, cream puffs, or fresh or stewed fruits. Calorie watchers beware: French ice cream is usually the real thing, that is, it's made with real cream, whole eggs, and real sugar. Ask for nonfat *sorbet* (sohr-BAY) instead.

Pasta. *Pâtes* (paht) or *pâtes fraîs* (paht FRAY) or *nouilles* (NOO-ee). Pasta is often served as a side dish in France and sometimes as a first course. But don't expect to see much of the simple, light pasta dishes so prevalent in Italy, as French chefs usually like to anoint noodles with butter, cream, wild mushrooms, cheese, and other rich accompaniments.

Peanuts. *Cacahuètes* (kah-kah-WHETT). Salted peanuts can be found in supermarkets, at the corner café (look for them among the candy bars and cigarettes located near the cashier), and sometimes in your hotel minibar. For those of us who love peanut butter (which is fairly difficult to procure in France since the French don't seem to share our fondness for it), boxes of salted, roasted peanuts generally do the trick in terms of satisfying a craving.

Potatoes. *Pommes de terre* (POHM de TAIR). Spuds are ubiquitous throughout France and can be a satisfying reprieve after experimenting with odd vegetables and unfamiliar side dishes. French cooks prepare potatoes in numerous ways, and the classic preparations have specific names. Look for the following dishes throughout the country:

- *Pommes allumette* (POHM zahl-oo-MET). Deep-fried matchstick potatoes.
- *Pommes Anna* (POHM zah-NAH). Sliced, layered potatoes baked with butter.
- *Pommes dauphin* (POHM doh-FEEN). Deep-fried potato croquettes.
- *Pommes duchesse* (POHM doo-SHESS). Cooked mashed potatoes thickened with egg yolks, then piped or formed into small shapes and baked until golden brown.
- *Pommes au four* (POHM zoh-FOOR). Baked potatoes.
- *Pommes gaufrettes* (POHM gah-FRET). Potatoes cut into thin, waffle-shaped slices and fried.
- *Pommes à l'huile* (POHM sahl WHEEL). Warm potato salad dressed with olive oil.
- *Pommes Lyonnaise* (POHM LEE-oh-NAYZ). Potatoes sautéed with onions, a specialty of Lyones.
- *Pommes mousseline* (POHM moo-SLEEN). Mashed potatoes mixed with whipped cream.
- *Pommes nature* (POHM nah-TUHR) or *pommes à l'anglaise* (POHM zah lahn-GLAIZ). Peeled, steamed potatoes, sometimes served with a little butter and/or chopped parsley.

Roast. *Rôti* (ro-TEE). The word *rôti* means "roasted," signifying foods cooked in the oven. Roasts (e.g., chicken, beef, lamb, and veal) are usually simply prepared and relatively unadorned, like the kinds of things Grandma used to make for Sunday lunch.

Salad. *Salade* (sa-LAHD). Travelers often crave vegetables, and a delicious way to satisfy that hunger is with a salad. Although there are some French salads that constitute a meal, cafés and brasseries will be happy to serve you one at lunch, but not at dinner, when you are expected to dine like the French, that is, having your salad *after* the main course to clear the palate. Some specialty salads to look for:

- *Salade frisée aux lardons* (sa-LAHD FREE-say oh lahr-DOHN). A hearty, pleasantly bitter curly endive. *Frisée* is the perfect counterpoint to salty bacon (*lardons*) and a warm, tangy dressing.
- *Salad niçoise* (sa-LAHD nee-SWAZ). A substantial mix of green beans, tomatoes, potatoes, olives, capers, anchovies, tuna, and vinaigrette sauce.
- *Salade de Roquefort, noix et endives* (sa-LAHD deh rohk-FUHR, nwah zay ahn-DEEV). Pungent blue cheese, walnuts, and crisp Belgian endive make this a pleasing salad indeed, especially in cool weather, when the rich ingredients stick to the ribs.

Soup. *Soupe* (soop). There's nothing like a bowl of soup when you're tired, cold, or simply feeling out of sorts. Look for the word *soupe* on menus throughout France, but be aware that French soups can be very simple or very complex. A particularly satisfying soup that can be had throughout the country is potato and leek soup, *potage aux poireaux et pommes de terre* (poh-TAJH oh pwar-OH ay POHM deh TAIR), also known as *potage parmentier* (poh-TAJH PAR-MAHN-tee-AY). By either name, it is usually a simple, soothing mixture of leeks and potatoes in a brothy base. Other souplike dishes to look for include *garbure* (gahr-BUHR), an uncomplicated peasant dish made with cabbage, and *potée* (poh-TAY), which is similar to *garbure* but has pork and potatoes as well as cabbage. Both *garbure* and *potée* are hearty, warming, and fortifying, and need nothing more as an accompaniment than bread and a glass of wine. *Bouillabaise* (BOO-yah-BAZE) probably had humble beginnings as a fisherman's soup, but it has evolved into what is often an elaborate production, with several kinds of fish and shellfish. A *bisque* (bihsk) is generally thick, rich, and highly seasoned and is often made with pureed, cooked shellfish, such as lobster. If light, easy-to-digest fare is what you crave, don't order a bisque. If something rich and intense is what you're after, by all means, try the bisque. If the word *velouté* (veh-loo-TAY) is used to describe a soup, it's a tip-off that the soup is probably enriched with cream, milk, egg yolks, or all three. *Matelotes*, *meurettes*, and *pauchouses* (MAH-teh-LOTT, myuhr-ETT, pah-SHOOZ) are all hearty fish chowders, which vary from region to region but can usually suffice as a meal. *Bourride* (boo-REED) is a Provençal fish stew served with *aioli* (ah-oh-LEE), garlic-flavored mayonnaise. It's usually quite rich and assertive, not the thing to order if your stomach is out of sorts.

Stews and stewlike dishes. The words *ragoût* (rah-GOO) and *estouffade* (est-too-FAHD) signify what we know as stews, describing foods cooked slowly over a low flame, yielding tender textures and deep, complex flavors. Also look for *blanquettes* (blahn-KETT) of veal or lamb as well as *osso bucco* (ah-so-boo-koh), veal shanks simmered until fork-tender, an Italian favorite that is also beloved in France. *Daubes* (dohb) and *pot-au-feu* (PO-toh-FUH) are meaty dishes that will remind the traveler of Mom's pot roast. *Poule-au-pot* (POO-loh-POH) is stewing chicken simmered in broth. Another word to look for is *fricassé* (FREE-kah-SAY), which is usually a mildly flavored stew-type dish made of chicken or veal in a creamy sauce.

REGIONAL/SEASONAL
SPECIALTIES

· ■ ·

To THE uninitiated the term "French food" usually
conjures up images of rich pâtés, buttery croissants,
and sauces thickened with cream. Those foods are
indeed part of the Gallic repertoire, but so are
sauerkraut and sausages, pizzalike savory pies, low-
fat cheeses, and hearty buckwheat pancakes. Not
only is French fare varied, but as in most of the
world, the menu changes from region to region.
Some dishes—such as the Provençale chickpea-
flour crepes known as *socca*—are usually found only
in certain parts of France. Other dishes—like *potée*
or *garbure*, which hail from Lorraine and Gascony,
respectively—are found on tables all over France but
vary according to the local market basket. For the
most part, there are certain dishes that are better,
fresher, or more authentic when consumed in their
place of origin. This summary of regional specialties is designed to help the traveler eat well by en-
joying the best that each region has to offer.

France can be divided into roughly a dozen culinary regions, which are distinguished by topography and climate. The lay of the land and the weather influence farming, fishing, and lifestyle and, therefore, cuisine. The French are fiercely proud of their native dishes, and there are strict laws that protect the usage of place-names to describe certain foods. For example, the term *Roquefort* can only be used for the blue-veined cheese from the town of Roquefort. Likewise, chickens bred and raised by the strict standards in the town of Bresse are the only chickens that can be labeled *Bresse.* In a similar manner, in the U.S.A. we use geographical terms to describe the quality of certain foods like Texas beef, Carolina barbecue, and a Jersey tomato.

In terms of seasonal specialties, some things go almost without saying, as they have the same harvest dates as they do in the States: peaches, plums, apricots, and cherries in summer; wild mushrooms, game, apples, pears, and grapes in autumn and winter; asparagus, strawberries, and rhubarb in spring. There are certain specialties that are unique to France, however, and many are related to the holidays: Bûche de Noël at Christmas, chocolates shaped like fish for April first, and many others. Certain holiday celebrations also have special names, such as Réveillon, which refers to dinner served at Christmas Eve and New Year's Eve gatherings.

What follows is a summary of regional specialties so the traveler may enjoy what each area does best.

BRITTANY

Bordered by the English Channel, the Bay of Biscay, and the Atlantic Ocean, this region has a long coastline dotted with numerous fishing ports that provide France with much of its fish and shellfish. Breton oysters (*huître*) (specifically, *spéciaux, Bélon, Creuse,* and *papillon*) are prized throughout the country, as are lobsters, mussels, clams, scallops, crabs, and sea urchins. The traveler is also encouraged to try the local sole, turbot, and sea bass as well as the local fish stew, *cotriade.* (Suprisingly, dishes described as *à la bretonne* refer not to fish or shellfish but to foods served with white beans. *À la bretonne* can also refer to sauce made with white wine, carrots, and celery.) Crepes—sometimes made with buckwheat flour—are a specialty of the region and can be enjoyed simply (with a smear of sweet butter) or with substantial fillings like ham, cheese, and scrambled eggs. (In Brittany, crepes are also known as *galettes*.) And what to drink with your crepes? Why, the local *cidre* (apple cider), of course. But be aware that in France, *cidre* contains alcohol; for a nonalcoholic apple drink, try *jus de pomme* (apple juice) instead. (For more information about cider, see Beverages A to Z: Cider.) If you're hankering for something sweet while in Brittany, don't miss *gâteau breton*, a rich dessert similar to pound cake; *kouign-amann*, a sweet yeast cake; and *sablés bretons*, buttery sugar cookies. As for cheeses, Brittany is not famous for any, except perhaps for *crémet nantais*, a fresh, creamy-tasting unsalted farmer's cheese, often served with whipped cream.

NORMANDY

The English Channel borders Normandy to the north and provides the region with fresh turbot, halibut, hake, bream, dab, and monkfish. But it is Dover sole that is the prize catch, esteemed by chefs for its fine, firm texture and delicate flavor. Norman cooks prepare it in a variety of ways; one of the best is also the simplest: *à la meunière,* lightly dusted with flour and sautéed in butter.

Normandy has acres and acres of rich pastureland used for cattle. The result? Tripe that is said to be the best in France (look for *tripes à la mode de Caen,* which are prepared with carrots, onions, and cider and were made famous in the town of Caen) and dairy products that are known all over the world. Another result of all this pastureland is an excellent cheese selection. Local cheeses to try include *camembert, pont-l'Evéque, pavé d'Auges, Livarot, Neufchâtel,* and *Brillat-Savarin* (see Market Buying Tips: *Fromageries*). Dessert lovers should savor anything made with Normandy apples *(pommes),* including *tartes* (tarts) and *beignets de pommes à la normande* (apple fritters). Dishes described *à la normande,* in fact, refer to the addition or garnish of apples or apple products like cider and Calvados, distilled apple brandy (see Beverages A to Z.)

CHAMPAGNE, THE NORTH, AND
THE ÎLE DE FRANCE

Even though this region has a relatively short coast-line, the port town of Boulogne reins in a good portion of France's fish and shellfish. The local catch includes herring, sardines, oysters, and Boulogne mussels (these mussels are said by some to be the best in the world). Belgium borders the region to the east, so the traveler will find foods with Belgian and Flemish heritage, including Belgian endive (called simply *endive* in France) and dishes prepared *à la flamande*, which usually refers to foods prepared with cabbage, carrots, turnips, potatoes, and bacon. Other specialties include *gaufres* (waffles), *carbonnade de boeuf à la flamande* (braised beef with beer), and *flamiche* (a quichelike vegetable tart).

Notable cheeses of the region include Chaource, maroilles, brie de Melun, and brie de Meaux (see Market Buying Tips: *Fromageries*). Travelers will also find excellent pork products here, including *andouillettes*, *pâtés*, *boudins*, and ham. Cabbage grows well in Champagne, and one finds it on the tables of country restaurants as well as fancy ones crossing all socioeconomic barriers. And what about that bubbly beverage? When used in cooking, champagne's bubbles and alcohol dissipate, leaving only the flavor. But oh what a flavor! Restaurants and pastry shops feature sweet regional specialties like *tarte au sucre* (yeast cake with sugar topping) and *anglois* (plum tart) that should not be missed. The Île de

France—roughly, Paris and its environs—was once composed of rich farmlands and was famous for asparagus (from Argenteuil), cream (from Chantilly), cherries (from Montmorency), carrots (from Crécy), and peas (from St. Germaine). Today, the area around Paris that once provided the city with produce is largely comprised of suburban neighborhoods.

THE LOIRE

This region—named for the river that runs through it—lies southwest of Paris and is easily accessible from the City of Lights by car or train. The Loire is a popular tourist destination because of the fairy-tale castles that dot the landscape. And while there, the traveler can also enjoy one of France's most elegant regional cuisines and extraordinary local wines. The Loire River is the longest river in France and is abundant with fish, including pike, mullet, bream, and eel, which, not surprisingly, all find their way into the local cuisine. Salmon and shad have always been an important part of the diet here, but the fishing of both is now regulated. However, they still appear on menus throughout the Loire because they have always been a local favorite. Cooks have a great respect for the naturally good flavors of the catch of the day, so fish are often prepared very simply—grilled, broiled, sautéed—and served with sauces or accompaniments that will enhance—not hide—the flavor. *Sauce oseille* (sorrel sauce) and *heurre blanc* (butter sauce) are two regional favorites. The local catch frequently makes its way into the stewpot along with mushrooms, cream, and red wine to make *matelote*. For a delicious snack, try *friture*, tiny, deep-fried fish (usually whitebait or smelt) served in cafés throughout the region.

But there is much more to the Loire than fish. It's also known for game, mushrooms (wild and cultivated), and pork, which is often made into *rillettes*, a savory spread of cooked, shredded pork. Fruit is also memorable here. Because of the relatively temperate climate, fruit orchards abound in the Loire. Some outstanding varieties to look for include prunes from Tours, Reinette apples from Le Mans, and pears from Anjou. Not surprisingly, fruit tarts and fruit fritters celebrating the local riches are made throughout the region. Perhaps the most famous Loire dessert is *tarte tatin*, an upside-down caramelized apple tart. Two other local specialties are *tourteau fromage*, a not-too-sweet cheesecake with a characteristic blackened domelike upper crust and *gâteau de Pithiviers*, a rich, puff pastry pie with a creamy almond filling.

Even though very good butter and cream are produced in the Loire and are often added to sauces and soups, the region is not particularly famous for its cheeses. The two to try are *crémets* (a fresh, mild cheese often eaten with sugar and cream for dessert or mixed with fresh herbs for a savory spread) and *port-salut* a mild, semisoft cheese distinguished by its orange rind (see Market Buying Tips: *Fromageries*).

The region that includes Burgundy (Bourgogne) and the area around Lyons (known as the *Lyonnais*) is a food lover's paradise, known for its hearty, full-flavored fare and some of the world's most extraordinary wines. The region is southeast of Paris and has two rivers running through it: the Saône and the Loire. Burgundy is famous for tender beef from the ivory-colored Charolais cattle, *escargots* (snails), and hams cured from corn-fed pigs. Dijon is known for the tangy mustard that bears its name (*à la Dijon* or *Dijonnaise* usually denotes the presence of mustard) and also for crème de cassis, a sweet black currant liqueur often mixed with dry white wine (to make kir) or with champagne (for a kir royale). The wines of Burgundy flavor much of the region's food, including beef (for *boeuf bourguignonne*), chicken (*coq au vin*), eggs (*oeufs en meurette*), and fish (*pochouse*, or *pauchouse*, a freshwater fish stew). The term *à la bourguignon* usually refers to foods cooked with mushrooms, bacon, and small onions. As for drinking the wine, it is excellent with *gougère*, a savory pastry, and the local cheeses, which include *Saint-Florentin*, *bleu de Bresse*, and *époisses* (see also Market Buying Tips: *Fromageries*).

In Lyons, travelers should try quenelles, light, airy dumplings often made with fish or shellfish, and *saladier lyonnais*, which traditionally has *mâche* (soft salad greens), *trevise* (pleasantly bitter red lettuce), bacon, a soft-cooked egg, and anchovies. The region is also known for its *gratins*, especially *gratinée lyonnaise* (onion soup) and *pommes de terre lyonnaise* (sliced potatoes sautéed with onions), which are perhaps the region's most famous dishes and are available throughout France. (The term *à la lyonnaise* usually refers to a garnish of onions.) Lyons's best-known cheese is probably *Saint-Marcellin*, but *soumaintrain*, and *rogotte de Condrieu* are also tempting choices (see Market Buying Tips: *Fromageries*). For dessert, try the locally made macaroons, meringues, *bugnes* (sweet fritters), and chocolates, especially those from Lyons's most famous chocolate shop, Bernachon.

CENTRAL FRANCE

This area—known as *Le Centre* (leh SAHN-truh)—includes the provinces known as the Auvergne, the Bourbonnais, and Limousin. Since much of the region is mountainous (the Massif Central range lies in the southeastern part of this region), the cooking tends to be homey, generous, stick-to-the-ribs–type fare with cabbage, potatoes, and pork figuring prominently. In fact, dishes described as *à l'auvergnate* (in the style of the Auvergne) usually means they are prepared with cabbage, sausage, and bacon. Cheese is important, too. Central France is famous for its high-quality milk and cream, much of which becomes outstanding cheeses, including *cantal*, *Saint-Nectaire*, *bleu d'Auvergne*, and *fourme d'ambert* (see Market Buying Tips: *Fromageries*). Enjoy them with the local *pain de seigle* (rye bread), which comes in all shapes and sizes. A notable local dish that combines two mountain staples—the potato and cheese—is *aligot*, a hefty, creamy blend of mashed potatoes and a cheese of the same name (see Market Buying Tips: *Fromageries*). Another specialty of the region are the tiny, delicately flavored, dark green lentils from Le Puy, which are often added to soups or served with sausages or smoked ham.

THE PAYS BASQUE, GASCONY, AND THE PYRÉNÉES

The Pyrénées mountains, which separate France and Spain, form the southern border of this region; the Atlantic Ocean borders it to the west. The cooking of this area is mostly peasant-style, with bell peppers, cornmeal, and ham being major hallmarks. The *Pays Basque* (Basque country), which lies in the west and has the Atlantic Ocean as its border, features a diet that includes—among other seafood—tuna, swordfish, sardines, and anchovies. The local fish stew is called *ttoro*, which may include conger eel, hake, monkfish, mussels, and scampi along with tomatoes, white wine, and hot peppers. Another Basque favorite is salt cod, which is often served *à la basquaise*: soaked, simmered, flaked, and served with a sauce of bell peppers, tomatoes, and garlic. The dish that is most often used to define Basque cooking is *pipérade* (also called *pipérade basquaise* and *omelette aux piments*), a creamy, soft, bell pepper-and-egg mixture that is served throughout the region.

As is the case with other mountainous regions in the world, cornmeal is an important part of the diet. The traveler may find it in the countryside served as a porridge called *brove*, *millas*, or *las pous*. Like Italian polenta, this cornmeal porridge is often cooled, sliced, and sautéed, then served as a side dish. For snacking, enjoy the local sheep's milk cheeses, particularly *Ossau-Iraty*, which is considered one of the country's best (see Market Buying Tips: *Fromageries*). Regional sweets include *gâteau basque*, which has a sweet dough with a texture somewhere between cookie, piecrust, and cake— and a rich pastry cream filling flavored with anise, almonds, rum, or fruit. Another typical *basquaise* sweet is *touron*, or *ttouron*, an almond-flavored cake of Spanish origin.

Bayonne, a town near the Atlantic coast, is famous for its hams. The French enjoy it thinly sliced as a first course (like Italian prosciutto) and on sandwiches, as well as adding it to egg, rice, chicken, and vegetable dishes.

Gascony lies north of the Pyrénées and is known for its foie gras (liver from fattened geese and ducks) and for confit, which is usually served warm alongside potatoes sautéed in duck or goose fat. Gascony is the home of *garbure*, a hearty cabbage stew that usually has white beans plus salted or preserved goose, duck, or pork. Dishes described as *à la gasconne* often are foods that may contain ham, confit of duck or goose, or armagnac. For dessert, try the double-crust tarts and pies that are available throughout the region in various guises, including *croustade*, *tourtière*, and *pastis*. Whatever its name, it is essentially a relative of baklava, made of thin strudel dough filled with a sweetened prune or apple filling.

LANGUEDOC

This Mediterranean province is bordered by the Rhône River to the east, the Mediterranean Sea to the southeast, the Pyrénées and Spain to the south. It is, therefore, a diverse region in both terrain and gastronomy. Riches from the Mediterranean include sardines, lemon sole, red mullet, skate, octopus, scampi, mussels, and clams, some of which go into making *bourride*, the local fish stew, which is usually flavored with fennel, orange rind, and garlic, then thickened with egg yolks and aioli (garlic mayonnaise). Mussels from *Bouzigues* are also prized. The most famous Languedoc dish, however, is probably *cassoulet*, a rich concoction that is somewhat of a cross between a stew and a casserole. Cassoulet can include all or some of the following: duck, goose, garlic, mutton, pork, partridge, and sausage. It is, needless to say, hearty and filling and needs to be accompanied only by crusty bread, red wine, and a green salad.

The most famous cheese in Languedoc is *Roquefort*. There are so many imitations of this blue cheese—many of them not very good—that it is worth seeking out the real thing, which is creamy-yellow color with slate blue marbling. It has a buttery texture and pungent flavor and is delicious with a glass of sauterne to finish a meal. For something sweet, try *marrons glacés*, candied chestnuts. *Marrons*, the cultivated version of wild chestnuts (*chataîgnes*), are commercially produced in Languedoc.

PROVENCE

Provence is a veritable feast for the senses. It is the land of colorful landscapes and lively markets, where the perfume of lavender mingles with the aroma of pungent garlic. This is the place where soft sea breezes and brilliant sunshine soothe body and soul. It is also a place where food is anything but bland and subtle! Here, foods tend to be bold and highly seasoned, with capers, tomatoes, saffron, cayenne, garlic, and herbs, plus the local olives. Foods described as *à la provençale* usually refer to the addition of tomatoes, garlic, olives, eggplants, or anchovies. Neighboring Italy has influenced the table here and menus offer *pissaladière* (a savory, piz-zalike tart), *sauce pistou* (a basil, garlic, and olive oil *mélange* like the Italian pesto), *bagna cauda*, plus ravi-oli and other kinds of pasta. Provençale cooking in-cludes an abundance of fish and shellfish, including sea bass, mullet, monkfish, mussels, clams, sea urchins, sardines, squid, and langoustines. They are often seasoned with fennel, olives, and tomatoes or go into making bouillabaise, a full-flavored fish stew served with spicy *rouille* sauce, a puree of red pep-pers, garlic, egg yolks, olive oil, and tomato paste. Foods described as *l'arlesienne*, which means in the style of Arles, a town in Provence, are prepared with tomatoes, onions, eggplant, potatoes, rice, or olives.

Vegetable lovers should not miss *soupe au pistou* (vegetable soup served with a swirl of pesto sauce), *artichants à la barigoule*, or *ratatouille*, a blend of eggplant, zucchini, onion, and tomatoes. One of the region's tastiest treats is *socca*, thin chickpea-flour crepes available at just about any open-air market. Looking for a great sandwich? Try *pan bagna* (see Menu Primer A to Z.) Bread is particularly memorable in Provence, where bakeries show off loaves shaped like sunflowers (*pain d'Aix*) and which can be flavored with olive oil and lemon (*gibassier* or *pompe à l'huile*). There is also walnut bread (*pain aux noix*), olive bread (*pain aux olives*), aniseed bread (*pain à l'anis*), and more. Try them with local cheeses like *Picodon* or *Banon*. Still hungry? For dessert try *nougat* and *glacéed* fruits, the local confections.

ALSACE AND LORRAINE

This region in eastern France borders Belgium, Luxembourg, Germany, and Switzerland, and, not surprisingly, the cuisines reflects a Teutonic influence. In the hands of French chefs, however, traditional German fare becomes something entirely different indeed. The result is a distinctive cuisine unlike any other in the world.

Alsace, with the Vosges mountains to the west and the Rhine River to the east, is famous for such cabbage (*chou*) dishes as *Zewclwai* (a quichelike vegetable tart) and *Baeckeoffe* (a hearty meat and potato casserole). Other specialties to look for include *choucroute garnie* (sauerkraut with sausages), *Spaetzle* (dumplings), and *Flammekueche* (also called *tarte flambée*), which is similar to pizza, consisting of a thin dough topped with mild cheeses, bacon, and onions. And don't miss *coq au Riesling*, chicken cooked in the local white wine. Dishes described as *à l'alsacienne* usually include sauerkraut, sausage, and sometimes Riesling. For cheeses, *Munster* is king, and the traveler will find it much more distinctive than the bland, factory-made version available in the states. Enjoy it on sandwiches, salads, or all on its own. After dinner try one of the local eaux-de-vie; the most famous, perhaps, is kirsch, made from cherries.

Quiche Lorraine was named after the town in which it was born. Properly made—with real farm eggs, whole milk or cream, and *Gruyère* cheese—it is a far cry from the slack imitations served up in faux French restaurants in the rest of the world. Do try it here. Or, opt for *omelette Lorraine*, characterized by a filling of bacon, cheese, herbs, and cream. Although *potée* is eaten throughout France, the version from Lorraine may be the best known. Try this stew of salt pork, white beans, cabbage, and root vegetables for a taste of the French countryside. Also not to be missed while in Lorraine: *madeleines*—the little shell-shaped sponge cakes made famous by Proust—which originated in Commercy. Other musts for those with a sweet tooth: *pain de Gênes*—a rich, almond-flavored sponge cake—and almond macaroons from the town of Nancy, and *Kugelhopf*, a light yeast cake with nuts and dried fruits.

FRANCHE-COMTÉ, SAVOY, AND THE DAUPHINÉ

This region—bordered by the Alps and the Jura mountains to the east— is dairy country, and cheeses are famous here. When planning a mountain picnic, put the local specialties on your market list: *comté*, *beaufort*, *tomme*, and *reblochon*. The local cheeses are also enjoyed in many regional dishes, including salads, soups, and fondue. Walnuts grow well here and are used in many ways. The oil is used for cooking and in sauces and salad dressings; the nuts themselves are used in dessert making—especially in tarts—and to make a walnut-flavored brandy.

In the Alps, clear, unpolluted waters provide fishermen with carp, perch, and pike and the traveler is likely to see sauces and garnishes of crayfish, which is famous in Nantua. The mountains are also known for hearty fare like *gratins* (*gratin dauphinois*, sliced potatoes baked with milk and cheese, is especially renowned), cornmeal mush, *matefaim* (MAHT-fam), which is a pancakelike bread, and a host of soups. Looking for a regional dessert? Try *biscuit de Savoie* (a light sponge cake flavored with vanilla extract, lemon zest or juice, or orange flower water or anise), *regal savoyard* (a hazelnut-raspberry tart similar to Linzer torte), *tarte aux noix* (walnut tart), and *rissoles*, or turnovers.

THE SOUTHWEST

Meats, poultry—especially duck and geese—and fruits and vegetables are in good supply here, and, because of a long coastline along the Atlantic, fish are abundant, too, with prawns and oysters being especially noteworthy. The local fish chowder is *chaudrée*, a hearty meal in a bowl. The area of Charente is famous for its dairy products, especially butter, which is extolled by chefs in France and beyond. Walnuts grow well in the areas of Sarlat and Quercy, and the traveler may find *sauce aïllade*— a specialty of Perigord—made of garlic, walnuts, and oil—served as an accompaniment to duck breasts. *Foie gras* (of geese and duck) is also renowned here. Walnuts are also used to make a liqueur known as *Eau de Noix*; try it after dinner with a cup of espresso. A sauce described as *bordelaise* or *à la bordelaise* usually refers to the addition of red or white Bordeaux wine, but it can also refer to a sauce or garnish of wild mushrooms. Perigord is known for its truffles; travelers in the region during truffle season will no doubt find it on local menus. *Sauce perigueux* is a rich brown sauce with Madeira and truffles served with meat, game, poultry, and eggs. Such dishes may also be called *à la périgourdine* or just *perigueux*. As for cheeses, the locals eat mostly *Edam*, a tradition dating back to the 1700s, when the Dutch traded cheese for wine. If you do come across a goat cheese called *chabichou*, do try it. It's mild when young and fresh and becomes more pungent as it ages (see Market Buying Tips: *Fromageries*). Satisfying a sweet tooth in this region is easy; try the *macarons* from Saint-Émilion or *merveilleuses*, sweet fritters flavored with cognac.

MARKET BUYING TIPS

· ■ ·

FOR FOOD lovers, marketing in France can be as much fun as a trip to the Louvre or shopping for designer shoes. If you've only shopped in American grocery stores, chances are that perusing the shelves of a French bakery (*boulangerie*), chocolate shop (*chocolaterie*), cheese shop (*fromagerie*), or candy shop (*confiserie*) will be a memorable experience indeed. (And for purists, there are shops featuring organic, or *biologique*, foods.)

Obviously, going to food shops and markets is the way to find sustenance for a train ride, a picnic, or a snack in your hotel room. But even if you don't intend to eat anything anywhere but in a restaurant, a visit to the various food shops is highly recommended. The variety of cheeses, the freshness of the produce, and the scent of fresh-baked bread are all part of the French experience, as much as (or maybe even more so) seeing the *Mona Lisa*, shopping at Chanel, or visiting the beaches of Normandy. Buying food at the *marché* (open-air market) is fairly straightforward: Point to (or ask for) what you want; then pay the vendor. Actual food shops are a little different. Often you ask for (or point to) what you want, at which point the salesclerk will give you a ticket. Take the ticket to the *caisser* (cashier) at the *caisse* (cash desk) and pay the required amount. Take your receipt *back* to the salesclerk, who will give you your wine/olives/bread or whatever. Note: The word *tranche* means slice; the word *émincé* means thinly sliced. Use them, if necessary, to describe how much ham or cheese you want.

There are several kinds of places to shop for food in France. There are outdoor markets—*marchés* (marshay)—in nearly every town on certain days of the week. This is where you'll see what the locals eat. In Brittany, there are mussels and oysters; in Provence, *glacéed* fruits, garlic, basil, and lavender honey; in Alsace, Munster cheese, cabbage in varying shades of green and purple, various kinds of sausages; and so on. By visiting the outdoor markets, one can get a sense of the region's geography and climate simply by looking at what is available in the various stalls. And for a bit of sociology, watch the shoppers carefully peruse the stands, looking for tiny new potatoes that are just the right size and shape for whatever stew or roast is planned for dinner. Just remember: Don't touch! Unlike American farmers' markets, in France the shopper is not supposed to pick up, poke, or squeeze the produce. If you want to buy something, you have to ask for it. And if you feel shy about your language skills, simply point to what you want. Handling the produce will get you snarls and growls from the vendor for sure. But bear in mind that it isn't that the vendors are being unkind, they simply know that if their pretty plums, figs, or tomatoes are squeezed all day long, they'll get shopworn, and, in the end, it's the vendor who loses. Let the vendor choose your peaches.

To find out when the outdoor markets are open, ask the hotel's concierge. If you're shopping for a picnic or snack, take along a plastic shopping bag or a woven string bag when you go marketing, as bags aren't usually given with a purchase. The outdoor market is where you'll want to buy produce (you'll see varieties of apples, pears, plums, and grapes not grown in the U.S.A.), olives (there are many different types, some flavored with herbs, others with garlic). Outdoor markets may also sell live, or just-plucked, chickens, freshly caught fish, just-dug truffles, and newly laid eggs. Some really big markets will also sell racks of new clothes, shoes, cosmetics, and housewares. Others are almost like flea markets, with an antique section, where pretty, secondhand bed linens, handkerchiefs, and monogrammed napkins are sold. (These make great gifts back home by the way, since they're easy to pack, don't weigh much, and are unlike anything back in the States. And who knows? You may even find some linen pillowcases monogrammed with your initials!)

FOOD SHOPS

Before the days of refrigeration, most French cooks shopped every day for that night's dinner. Some foods in France are still best consumed the day they are bought (bread, for example), and it is not uncommon—even today—for the cook to pick up one or two things on the way home from work. Shops are separated by specialty, and sometimes the food itself is actually prepared on site. Planning a lunch in the park? You'll want to go to the bakery, deli, and pastry shop, plus maybe a wineshop and a cheese shop. And if you're really feeling indulgent, add a chocolate shop to your list. Food shops in France tend to be clustered—often they are located near the outdoor market—so you probably won't have to travel far to get everything you need. And as is the case with the farmers' market, take your own bags (the laundry valet bag in your hotel room will suffice), put the food in your backpack, or be prepared to pay for a bag. (Note: Very fancy shops will give you a bag free, but the food will be more expensive.)

The following shops are the standard in most French cities and towns. Included here is not only a description of what each shop is like but also a summary of some things you may want to purchase for a snack, a picnic, or to take back to the States.

Boulangeries (boo-lahn-JHREE)

The French bakery sells bread, of course, but not just any old bread—French bread! The clichéd image of a man wearing a beret on a bicycle carrying a long French loaf under his arm is not something that Hollywood made up; it's real! Stand outside the *boulangerie* and watch; you'll see schoolchildren with their nannies in the morning grabbing a quick roll, housewives picking up earthy loaves for a rustic supper, and private chefs purchasing fancy *petits pains* (PEH-tee pan) for a special dinner party. Walk inside, close your eyes, breathe in the fresh yeasty aromas. Open your eyes wide and feast on the spectacular array of baked goods. *Boulangeries* in large cities will offer many, many kinds; those in smaller cities will at least carry the basics, which include some or all of the following:

- *Baguette* (ba-GETT). A long, thin loaf of white bread. (See Menu Primer A to Z.)
- *Baguette au levain* (ba-GETT oh lay-VAHN). A sourdough baguette.
- *Baguettes moulées* (ba-GETT moo-LAY). Breads made of baguette dough baked in molds.
- *Bâtard* (BA-tahrd). Similar to a baguette but shorter and wider, good for slicing crosswise.
- *Boule* (bool). A round, ball-like loaf.
- *Brioche* (bree-OHSH). A yeast bread enriched with butter and eggs. (See Menu Primer A to Z.)
- *Croissant* (kwah-SAHN). A flaky, buttery, crescent-shaped pastry. (See Menu Primer A to Z.)
- *Ficelle* (fee-SELL). A long, thin loaf, similar to a baguette but slimmer and therefore crisper.
- *Fougasse* (foo-GAHSS). A flat, crisp-crusted bread that may be seasoned with herbs or spices.

- *Gibassier* (jhee-BAH-see-ay). Bread flavored with lemon and olive oil. (See Regional/Seasonal Specialties: Provence.)
- *Miche* (meesh). A large, roundish, rustic-style loaf.
- *Pain à l'anis* (pan ah lah-NEES). Bread flavored with aniseed. (See Regional/Seasonal Specialties: Provence.)
- *Pain biologique* (PAN bee-OH-lah-JHEEK). Bread made with organically grown and/or organically produced ingredients.
- *Pain de campagne* (PAN deh kahm-PAN-yah). Country-style bread that is usually made from baguette dough and is plump and round in shape.
- *Pain complet* (PAN kom-PLEH). Whole-wheat bread.
- *Pain de mie* (PAN deh MEE). Firm, white, sandwich-type bread. This can be purchased sliced or unsliced. (The shopkeeper can slice it for you—mechanically—in seconds.)
- *Pain aux noix* (PAN oh NWAH). Bread made with walnuts or hazelnuts. This bread is often served with the cheese course along with sweet butter.
- *Pain aux olives* (pan oh-zah-leev). Bread with olives.
- *Pain aux raisins* (PAN oh ray-SAHN). Bread made with raisins.
- *Pain de siègle* (PAN deh see-EHG-luh). Rye bread.
- *Parisienne* (pah-REE-see-EHN). A big loaf that is as long as a baguette but wider.
- *Pompe à l'huile* (pohmp ah LWHEEL). Bread flavored with olive oil and lemon. (See Regional/Seasonal Specialties: Provence.)

Charcuteries (SHAR-koo-teh-REE)

Travelers planning a picnic will find much of what they need at the charcuterie. This establishment is similar to a delicatessen, in that it sells freshly prepared foods as well as cooked and cured meats plus packaged foods like mustard, olives, and capers. Charcuteries often have plastic spoons and forks, too, so if you don't mind eating out of the plastic container, you're set for a feast.

The word "charcuterie" literally means "cooked meats," which are indeed a specialty of the shop. Many of the meats sold at the charcuterie such as hard, spicy cooked sausages called *saucisson* (kind of like salami), pâtés, and dry-cured hams, will travel well. Charcuteries usually also sell smoked salmon, meat, and vegetable terrines and an array of prepared salads. The charcuterie is also where many busy working people stop on their way home from the office to pick up ready-made foods for dinner. Some can be eaten as they are; others may require a quick zap in the microwave. (Yes, the French like convenience, too.) Some charcuteries also sell bread, wine, cheese, and pastries, so they can be a convenient stop if you are very hungry, very tired, and don't have time to go to four or five different shops.

When buying ham, pâté, or a terrine, ask for a *tranche* (transh), which means "slice," or demonstrate with your hands what size piece you want. After buying food for your picnic, poke around and look for gifts to take back to the States, such as attractively packaged bottles of vinegar, oil, honey, and olives.

What follows is a list of the most typical offerings of meat at the basic *charcuterie*.

Ballottine (BAH-loh-TEEN). Poultry, meat, fish, or game that has been boned, stuffed, rolled, and roasted. *Ballotines* are delicious sliced and served cold or at room temperature.

Galantine (GAH-lahn-TEEN). Poultry that has been cooked, boned, and stuffed or meat that has been stuffed and rolled. This is then cooked, sliced, and served cold.

Jambon cru (jham-BOHN KROO). Raw, cured ham, similar to Italian prosciutto. It is very good for sandwiches; try it on sliced *baguettes* spread with brie.

Jambon fumé (jham-BOHN foo-MAY). Smoked ham. Delicious with melon or for snacking.

Jambon persillé (jham-BOHN per-see-YAY). A specialty of Burgundy that consists of cold, cooked ham cut into cubes and put into a mold with parsley-flecked gelatin. The mold is then chilled to congeal the mixture, which is then sliced and served cold.

Pâté (pah-TAY). Finely ground or minced meat— usually pork— that has been mixed with spices and herbs, then baked. It is then sliced and served cold or at room temperature.

- *Pâté de campagne* (pah-TAY deh kahm-PAN-yuh). Coarse, "country-style" pâté that is usually made with pork and served with little pickles called *cornichons*.
- *Pâté de canard* (pah-TAY deh kah-NARD). With duck.
- *Pâté en croûte* (pah-TAY on KROOT). Baked in pastry.
- *Pâté de foie gras* (pah-TAY deh FWAH GRAH). With liver, usually goose or duck (foie gras means "fatted liver," referring to the over-sized and very delicious organ that results when geese or ducks are force-fed.)
- *Pâté de lapin* (pah-TAY dch lah-PAN). With rabbit.
- *Pâté de maison* (pah-TAY deh may-SOHN). "In the house style," usually that particular shop's own recipe.
- *Pâté de oie* (pah-TAY deh wah). With goose.

Rillettes (ree-YETT). A spread made of finely minced pork, goose, or duck that is cooked and served on bread or toast. (Do not eat this cold, as the fat will be congealed.)

Saucisson (SO-see-SOHN). Usually, air-dried sausage eaten sliced as a snack, like salami. It's terrific for picnics; just remember to take along a strong, sharp Swiss Army knife to slice it!

Terrine (TAY-reen). The term refers to an earthenware vessel used to cook meat, fish, poultry, or vegetable mixtures. It also refers to the food that is cooked in the vessel. Usually, the mixture is sliced in the vessel, then removed to serve.

Chocolateries (shoh-KOH-lah-tah-REE)

French chocolate shops are to the chocolate lover what the Louvre is to the art lover, something that upon entering almost overwhelms you with magnificence. Once inside a chocolate shop, the chocolate lover is likely to feel elation and awe. (And even those who don't care much for chocolate will at the very least find the place interesting.) The *chocolaterie* is the place to go to satisfy a craving for something deep, dark, and delicious.

You'll see lots of clear glass cases filled with dark, white, bittersweet, and milk chocolate in many forms: bars, truffles, plain pieces, filled pieces, chocolates stuffed with creams, dotted with nuts, or imprinted with designs. They're enough to weaken even the most stalwart dieter. And why resist? The French take their chocolates very seriously, and although the Swiss might argue, most chocoholics consider French chocolates to be the best in the world. Just remember, most filled chocolates are preservative-free and are meant to be consumed within a few days, while they're at their best.

Big-city *chocolateries* generally carry other fine sweets, too, that one can lump into the category of *confiseries* (KOHN-fee-seh-ree), or confections. These sweets include *marrons glacés* (MAH-rohn gla-say), candied chestnuts, and *pâtes de fruits* (PAHT deh fwee), fruit-flavored jellies that taste like sweetened fruit essences. If you have a sweet tooth, try both of these old-fashioned sweets. And if you like nuts, try *dragées* (DRAH-jhay), sugared almonds.

Chocolate Terms

Chocolat (SHOH-koh LAH). Chocolate.

Chocolat amer (SHOH-koh-LAH tah-mair) or *chocolat noir* (SHOH-koh-LAH nwahr). Bittersweet chocolate or dark chocolate.

Chocolat au lait (SHOH-koh-LAH toh lay). Milk chocolate. High-quality French milk chocolate is much finer than the factory-produced bars in the U.S.A. Try it, and bring back a few bars for the children on your shopping list.

Chocolat mi-amer (SHOH-koh-LAH mee-ah-mair). Bittersweet chocolate that is sweeter than *chocolat amer*. A good eating chocolate.

Couverture (KOO-vehr-TUHR). This type of chocolate is meant for cooking. If you like making chocolates at home, you may want to go to a specialty food store or kitchenware shop for this type of chocolate. While it is great for dipping truffles, it is not the best chocolate for eating on its own.

A note on white chocolate: White chocolate is not really chocolate, in that it contains no chocolate liquor (a dark liquid made by combining fermented, dried, and ground cocoa beans with cocoa butter, a natural vegetable fat from the cocoa bean). What we know as white chocolate is made with cocoa butter, sugar, milk solids, lecithin, and vanilla.

In addition to bars, truffles, and other confections, the *chocolaterie* may also carry powdered cocoa for making hot chocolate. If you—or someone you love—has a passion for that devilishly good chocolate drink, by all means buy one—or several—tins of cocoa to take home with you. And, speaking of gifts, most *chocolateries* have packaged gift boxes of chocolates that make terrific presents.

Fromageries (fro-MAH-jhe-REE)

Going to a cheese shop is a must for the food lover. The French probably produce more kinds of cheese than any other country in the world, and it is a food of which they are intensely proud. There are cheeses made of cow's milk, sheep's milk, and goat's milk. There are cheeses so young—barely fermented, in fact—that they're soft, sweet, and mild. There are cheeses that are dry and crumbly and others that are down-right gooey. Some have fuzzy blue-gray mold, some are coated in herbs or ash, others are wrapped in chestnut leaves. There are spoonable cheeses and cheeses that must be cut with the cheese monger's big strong knife. Try as many different kinds of cheese as you can while in France because most of the French cheeses sold in the States are made with pasteurized milk. Most French cheeses sold in France are made with unpasteurized milk and cannot be exported to the U.S.A. unless they are aged for over sixty days. Therefore, the "French" cheeses sold in the States tend to be somewhat blander and lacking in character than the real thing.

The Cheese Course

When you eat in a private home or a restaurant in France, you are often offered cheese after dinner. This tradition is alive and well, even in an era of cholesterol scares and calorie watching. However, whereas years ago diners might eat cheese *and* a dessert course, it seems to be more and more commonplace for the health-conscious diner to opt for one or the other. If you don't have a sweet tooth, cheeses are the ticket; they're rich and opulent, indulgent, and nice to enjoy with your last few sips of wine.

At the Cheese Shop

Most of the cheeses you buy should be consumed within a few days. If you do have cheeses left over from your picnic, store them in the paper they were wrapped in by the cheese monger and place them in a cool place in your hotel room. If the room is particularly warm, put the cheese on the lowest shelf (it's the warmest) of the minibar. Just remember to bring the cheese to room temperature *before* eating it; cheese is much more flavorful when eaten at room temperature than it is either warm or cold.

Here are some of the most popular French cheeses plus some personal favorites:

Aligot (ah-lee-GOHT). The fresh, white, spongy curds of *cantal* or *salers* cheese, which are usually served in a dish also called *aligot* (a mixture of the cheeses and mashed potatoes). It is a specialty of the Auvergne.

Banon (bah-NON). A small, round cheese made from cow's or goat's milk named after the northern Provencal town of Banon. The cheese is traditionally wrapped with chestnut leaves and tied with rafia. When young, it is a medium-mild cheese; as it ages, it becomes more assertive in flavor. It is often served at the end of meals, but it's good for snacking, too.

Beaufort (bo-FOHR). From the Savoy region, this creamy cow's milk cheese is mildly salty and somewhat fruity. It's delicious for snacks as well as for cooking, especially in fondue.

Bleu d'auvergne (bloo doh-VAIRN-yuh). From the mountains in the Auvergne region, this blue-veined cow's milk cheese is rather sharp in flavor. It's terrific after dinner with a big Rhône wine.

Bleu de Bresse (bloo deh BRESS). From Bresse in Burgundy, this blue-veined cow's milk cheese is rich, soft, and fairly assertive. Try it with a glass of Beaujolais.

Brie (bree). There are several different kinds of Brie, which are named after the villages near Paris where they are made. Brie de Meaux (bree deh MOH) and Brie de Melun (bree deh meh-LAHN) are the types you'll see in most *fromageries*. Bries are typically supple in texture and have a pleasant fragrance and a mild, fruity-tangy flavor. Brie spread on bread (instead of or *with* butter) and topped with razor-thin slices of dry, cured ham makes a delicious sandwich. It is also good eaten with fresh fruit as a snack.

Brillat-Savarin (bree-YAT sah-vah-RAN). A very rich, creamy, cow's milk cheese from Normandy that has a buttery texture and milky flavor. Enjoy it for dessert with fresh berries or peaches. The cheese is named for Anthelme Brillat-Savarin (1755–1826), the famous gastronome and author of *The Physiology of Taste*, a thoroughly enjoyable book all about food, eating, and tasting. It's a must for Francophiles and food lovers alike.

Cabecou (KAH-bay-koo). A small, disk-shaped cheese made of goat's or sheep's milk, sometimes wrapped in chestnut leaves. Cabecou is from the Southwest and is *not* imported into the U.S.A. Enjoy this soft creamy cheese in France—perhaps with a glass of Cahors, a dark red wine made from malbec grapes.

Camembert (KAM-uhm-bair). From Normandy, this soft cheese has a mild, fruity flavor with hints of mushrooms and is often served at the end of the meal. It's good for snacking, too.

Cantal (kahn-TAHL). From the Auvergne, this mild, nutty cow's milk cheese is often used in soups, sauces, and baked dishes such as *gratins*. It can also be enjoyed after a meal with a glass of light, fruity red wine.

Caprice des dieux (kah-PREES day DYUH). This rich, soft cheese is sold in a cardboard box with the name printed on it, so it's easy to spot. It is generally eaten at the end of the meal, but it's good for sandwiches and snacks, too. Since it's packaged, it's a good choice for picnics if you have to put lunch in your pack.

Chabichou (SHAH-bee-shoo). From Poitou in the Loire, this soft, cylindrical goat's milk cheese is delicious and worth seeking out since it is unavailable in the U.S.A. If it's young, enjoy it with a chilled glass of sauvignon blanc. If the *chabichou* is aged, try a glass of *chinon*, a red wine from Touraine.

Chaource (sha-UHRS). From a village in Champagne, this cow's milk cheese is soft and rich, with a faint mushroom aroma and milky-fruity taste. It is traditionally eaten after meals, often with a glass of champagne.

Chèvre (SHEH-vruh). The word means "goat," but it also refers to the cheeses made from goat's milk. There are many, many different kinds of *chèvre*—

from mild and soft to pungent and dry—but all have the telltale taste of goat's milk. Note: Cheeses that include the words *chevrette*, *chevrine*, and *chevrotin* in their names are also made with goat's milk.

Comté (kohm-TAY), also known as *Gruyère de comté* (groo-YAIR deh kohm-TAY). Made in the Jura mountains, this is considered the finest of the French *Gruyère* cheeses. Note: *Gruyère* is an area in Switzerland, and only true *Gruyères* are from that area. But the French use the term to identify a family of cheeses that are mild and hard and share a fruity-nutty flavor. Other "French" *Gruyères* include *beaufort* and *Emmenthal*). This is a good snacking and sandwich cheese and, since it is firm, a good choice for a warm-weather picnic.

Coulommiers (KOO-lohm-YAY). A cow's milk cheese from a town near Paris of the same name. *Coulommiers* has a soft, buttery, and slight mushroom flavor.

Crémets (kreh-MEH). Fresh, mild cow's milk cheese from the Loire, often eaten as dessert with fresh fruit and sugar. It is sometimes used to make *cour à la creme*, a creamy, molded, heart-shaped dessert, usually garnished with berries.

Crottin (kro-TAHN). Small, tangy, barrel-shaped goat's cheese from Burgundy. (The word *crottin* in French means "dung," which is what the cheeses are said to resemble in shape.) Enjoy these tasty little cheeses with a cool glass of Sancerre.

Emmenthal (EH-mahn-TAHL). A partially skimmed cow's milk cheese that is semifirm and has large holes. Look for *Emmental Gran Cru* on the rind, assuring that the cheese was made with Alpine milk. Delicious for snacking and sandwiches.

Époisses (ay-PWAHZ). A soft, buttery cow's milk cheese from Burgundy that has a rather spicy, tangy flavor. Delicious with a glass of red wine from the same region.

Explorateur (eks-PLOH-rah-TUHR). A very rich, buttery cow's milk cheese with a rather bold, creamy flavor.

Fourme d'ambert (FORM dahm-BAIR). A blue-veined cow's milk cheese from the Auvergne with a slight cedary aroma and rather assertive flavor.

Fromage blanc (FROH-majh BLAH). A fresh, soft, low-fat cow's milk cheese often eaten with fresh fruits. *Fromage blanc* is similar in taste to cottage cheese.

Langres (LAHN-gruh). A rich, spicy cow's milk cheese from Champagne.

Livarot (LEE-vah-RO). A soft cow's milk cheese from Normandy with a strong, spicy flavor. It is always packed in a wooden box, so consider it for backpack picnics. Try it with apples or apple cider.

Maroilles (mah-ROLL). A soft cow's milk cheese from the North (near Belgium) with a strong bouquet and tangy taste. Deliciously strong, not for the faint-hearted.

Mimolette (ME-moh-LETT). A rather firm cow's milk cheese from the North (and Normandy) with a clean, nutty flavor. Good for snacking.

Montrachet (MOHN-trah-SHAY). True, original *Montrachet* is a soft goat's milk cheese from Burgundy with a mild creamy taste. It is traditionally wrapped in grape leaves. The *Montrachet* wrapped in plastic— the kind exported to the U.S.A.—can be pleasant, but it's not as tasty as the genuine thing.

Morbier (MOHR-be-YAY). A cow's milk cheese from the Franche-Comté, it has a rather pleasantly aggressive, nutty flavor and is good for snacking. Try it with crisp, tart apples. *Morbier* is easy to identify because it has a thin line of charcoal (tasteless and edible) running through it.

Munster (MUHN-ster). This cow's milk cheese is a specialty of Alsace. It is soft and supple and has a somewhat spicy, tangy flavor. Good with Alsatian wines or for sandwiches and snacking.

Neufchâtel (NEHF-sha-TELL). A cow's milk cheese from Normandy with a smooth texture and a mild, savory, slightly salty taste. Delicious with red Bordeaux wines.

Ossau-Iraty (OH-soh EE-rah-TEE). An exceptional sheep's milk cheese from the Pyrénées with a fruity-nutty flavor. Enjoy it with a full red wine.

Pavé d'auges (PAH-vay dohjh). A squarish cow's milk cheese from Normandy. Creamy, rich, and delicious with cold cider or fresh apples.

Picodon (pee-koh-DAWN). There are several kinds of *Picodon*, a goat's milk cheese named after the region of Picodon, on the Rhône river. One of the most popular comes from Provence. This creamy goat's milk cheese is sweet and mild when young and becomes drier and more assertive with age. It is often sold packed in olive oil and herbs. Delicious with a glass of a "big" red wine.

Pont-l'Évêque (POHN lah VEK). A soft, slightly runny cow's milk cheese from Normandy. It's always sold in a wooden box. Try it with Normandy cider, as the locals do, or with apples or pears.

Port-salut (POHR sah-LOO). A mild cow's milk cheese from Brittany, available at every supermarket in France. If you are traveling with children, this nonassertive cheese is a good choice for snacks.

Reblochon (REH-blo-SHOHN). A soft cow's milk cheese from the Savoy with a mild, creamy flavor. Delicious with fresh fruits or a glass of young, fruity wine.

Rigotte (ree-GOHT). There are several kinds of *rigotte*. Most are made of cow's milk, but some are pure goat's milk, such as the rich, fragrant, *rigotte de Condrieu* (ree-GOHT deh kohn-dree-yuh) from the Lyonnais. Do try it if you travel to the region; it is delightful with a glass of wine—a *Condrieu*—from the same region.

Roquefort (rohk-FOR). A rather soft, crumbly, blue-veined cheese from a village in the Southwest of the same name. It's made from sheep's milk and is traditionally served at the end of the meal (sometimes with a glass of sauterne) but is also good on salads, toast, and some sandwiches.

Saint-Florentin (sahn FLO-rehn-TAN). A soft, full-flavored cow's milk cheese made in Burgundy. It is not exported to the U.S.A., so enjoy it here, with a glass of Burgundy, of course.

Saint-Marcellin (sahn MAHR-se LAN). A small goat's or cow's milk cheese made near Lyons, *Saint-Marcellin* is rather mild-tasting, tangy, and moderately salty.

Saint-Nectaire (SAHN nek-TAIR). A cow's milk cheese from the Auvergne usually served at the end of the meal or used for making cheese toast. It is soft and rather mild.

Soumaintrain (soo-mahn-TRAN). A very rich, creamy cow's milk cheese from Burgundy. It is not exported to the U.S.A.

Tomme (tohm). There are many kinds of *tomme*. Some are from cow's milk, others from goat's milk. Probably the best-known *tomme* is from the Savoy region and is called *tomme de Savoie*, which is rather firm in texture with a mildly salty, earthy taste.

Vacherin (VASH-uh-RAN). A very creamy, assertive cow's milk cheese from the Jura mountains in Franche-Comté. Recognizable by the band of spruce bark that surrounds it.

Pâtisseries (PAH-tee-suh-REE)

French pastries are frivolous, fattening, and fun. If you want to feel like a kid again, duck into a pâtisserie in a big French city. Even if you don't have a sweet tooth, the endless variety of cakes, tarts, cookies, and pastries will fill you with delight. The shiny glazes on bite-sized fruit tartlettes make them look like little jewels or miniature stained-glass windows; flat sugary *palmiers* look like something out of a fairy tale, and puffy éclairs—oozing with cream fillings—will leave even the most disciplined dieter weak in the knees. The vast selection of pastries are testimony to the fact that, indeed, the French love sweets. Ask yourself, "But why aren't they fat?" The answer is this: It seems to be partially genetic, but it's also an issue of how *often* and how *much* they eat. Generally speaking, most adults in France do not regularly eat desserts; they watch their waistlines just as we do. When they *do* eat sweets, however, you can bet that it's something rich, yummy, and delicious, not some kind of overly processed, factory-made confection filled with fake sugar, fake fat, and fake salt. The idea is this: If you have something *really* delicious, you will be satisfied with a small portion and won't seek fulfillment in volume.

The French rely heavily on the local pâtisserie for home entertaining, holiday feasts, and for sugar fixes in general. French pastry chefs have perfected the art of baking, and most busy Frenchmen and Frenchwomen simply don't have time to fuss around with buttery dough and cream puffs. Besides, why make éclairs when you can buy them down the street at the pâtisserie?

Here are some of the most popular offerings:

Brioche (BREE-ohsh). A yeast bread enriched with butter and eggs. (See Menu Primer A to Z.)

Croissant (KWAH-sahn). A flaky, buttery, crescent-shaped pastry. (See Menu Primer A to Z.)

Financiers (FEE-nahn-see-AY). A tiny, buttery-rich cake. (See Menu Primer A to Z.)

Gâteau Basque (GAH-toh bask). A cake. (See Regional/ Seasonal Specialties: The Pays Basque, Gascony, and the Pyrénées.)

Gâteau opéra (GAH-toh oh-PAY-rah). A cake. (See *Opéra* in Menu Primer A to Z.)

Madeleines (mah-dah-LAHN). Small, light, shell-shaped sponge cake.

Pain au chocolat (PAH-noh SHOH-koh-LAH). A rich, flaky yeast dough—such as that used in making croissants— wrapped around a semisweet chocolate bar. Rich, delicious, and a must if you're traveling with children.

Palmier (pahlm-YAY). A crisp, cookie-type sweet. (See Menu Primer A to Z.)

Pithiviers (pee-TEE-vee-AY). A rich, puff pastry dessert. (See Menu Primer A to Z.)

Quatre-quarts (KAHTR-kar). Pound cake. (See Menu Primer A to Z.)

Tarte tatin (tahrt tah-TAN). An upside-down apple pie. (See Menu Primer A to Z.)

Tourteau Fromage (TOOR-toh FRO-majh). A not-too-sweet cheesecake made from goat's cheese that is a specialty of Poitou-Charentes in the Southwest.

Specialty Food Shops

There are other shops in France—particularly in the bigger cities, like Paris, Lyons, and Bordeaux—where a variety of fancy foods are sold. These shops—sometimes called *épiceries* (ay-PEE-seh-REE)—are really sophisticated grocery stores since they may carry everything from the best-quality butter and cream to the most perfect peaches just imported from another continent. Plus there will often be exotic mushrooms, teas, coffees, herbs, spices, honey, olives, and a variety of sweets. Some shops may also have a takeout section offering prepared foods, many of which can be part of a delicious picnic or snack in the hotel room. These specialty shops are a must if the traveler is shopping for fellow food lovers, for it is here that one can purchase exotic fruit vinegars, hazelnut and walnut oils, preserved goose liver pâté packed in tins, lovely little *de Puy* lentils, and more. A plus: These fancy shops usually wrap everything beautifully; just watch the shopkeeper lovingly tie ribbons around a box of macaroons. This is a feast in itself and evidence of the utter reverence the French have for fine food.

Note: Some of the most famous specialty food stores in Paris are:

- *Fauchon* (foh SHAWN), 26 place de la Madelaine.
- *Hédiard* (AY-dee-AHR), 21 place de la Madeleine.
- *Petrossian* (peh-TROH-see-EHN), 18 boulevard La Tour–Maubourg.

- *Soleil de Provence* (soh-LAY deh pro-VAHNS), 6 rue du Cherche-Midi.

WINESHOPS

Visiting a wineshop in France is a memorable experience for the wine lover, who will see bottles of wines that he or she has only read about in books. And the newcomer to wine will likely be in awe; the rows and rows of carefully stored bottles are cause for wonder indeed.

Before buying, brief yourself by looking at the wine section in the Beverage Primer, which will help you sort through the many, many wines you'll see on the shelves. In big cities, the salespeople will speak English. Note: Wine is also sold in specialty food stores, supermarkets, and often at the little neighborhood corner market. And if you're buying the wine to enjoy now, don't forget to buy a corkscrew—*tire bouchon* (teer boo-SHOHN)—if you forgot to pack one as most corkscrews on pocket knives usually don't perform as well as the real thing.

SUPERMARCHÉ

Even if you don't need to buy anything, a trip to the *supermarché* is an experience. It is here that you'll see what the average Frenchman buys and eats, from vacuum-packed, cooked new potatoes (that just need to be reheated for a minute or two before eating), to microwavable foods, to packaged cookies, crackers, and candies. You'll see some familiar foods, like American cold cereals, but the names and labels have been changed to seduce the French shopper. By looking at the supermarket staples, the traveler can see very quickly what is important to the French homemaker who doesn't regularly shop at fancy pastry shops or chocolate shops. The *supermarché* is also an excellent place to shop for reasonably priced food gifts to take home. Look for oils, vinegars, honey, olives, and chocolate bars, among other treats. Just don't expect the cashier to package your purchase in a fancy box tied with a bow as the fancy shops do. (Note: The *supermarché* also sells non-food items, just as American supermarkets do.)

COOKWARE SHOPS

Those who love to eat often love to cook. Even if cooking is not your passion, chances are you'll find cookware shops a fascinating stop. Cookware shops in the big cities feature shelves and shelves of chocolate molds, rolling pins, pastry bag tips, and cookie cutters. There will also be every kind of baking sheet, roasting dish, and knife imaginable. Those who love to bake shouldn't miss the stacks of pretty little tartlette tins, which come in just about every size imaginable. These goodies make terrific gifts for fellow cooks back home. And who knows, shopping here may just inspire you to do some cooking yourself.

USEFUL WORDS
QUICK REFERENCE GUIDE

· ■ ·

In the mood for lamb chops, but don't know how to say it in French? Allergic to crab, but don't know what the word is for that crustacean that leaves you covered in hives? Need a fork, some salt, or a menu? This A to Z listing can get you out of a jam or help you ask for some.

Allergies. *Allergies* (ah-lair-JHEE).

Almond. *Amande* (ah-MAHND). Almonds are used in dessert making throughout France.

Anchovy. *Anchois* (ahn-SHWAH). Anchovies are used a great deal in the cooking of southern France. The traveler will find them on *pissaladière* (see Regional/Seasonal Specialties: Provence) as well as in *tapenade* (see Menu Primer A to Z).

Appetizer. *Hors d'oeuvre* (or-DUHRV). These small, savory treats are usually served before the meal with an apéritif. Crudités and canapés fall into this category.

Apple. *Pomme* (pohm). Apples are a specialty of Normandy (see Regional/Seasonal Specialties: Normandy), where they are used, among other things, in making tarts and cider (see Beverages A to Z: Cider). But even though Normandy apples are perhaps the most famous in France, very good apples are found throughout the country.

Apricot. *Abricot* (ah-bree-KOH). Apricots are grown in Provence and Languedoc in southern France, where the growing season is long and the weather somewhat temperate. Fresh apricots are a delicious treat and can be found in most farmers' markets throughout the country. Apricots are used in making desserts, compotes, and jams.

Artichoke. *Artichaut* (AR-tee-SHOW). Artichokes grow in southern France, where they are enjoyed a number of ways, especially *à la barigoule* (see Menu Primer A to Z: *Artichauts à la barigoule*).

Asparagus. *Asperge* (ah-SPAIRJH). This elegant vegetable is a particular specialty of the Loire Valley, an area known as "the garden of France" because of the abundance of produce that is grown there. Asparagus is a labor-intensive crop, especially white asparagus, which grows completely under the soil because the sun turns this vegetable green. While white asparagus is considered more of a specialty item than green asparagus, both can be used interchangeably in recipes.

Avocado. *Avocat* (ah-voh-KAH).

Bacon. *Lardons* (lahr-DOHN). Bacon is not served in pan-fried strips for breakfast in France, but it is frequently diced, cooked, and served on salads or used to flavor soups, stews, and long-cooked dishes like *coq au vin*. Lardons add a deep, smoky flavor as well as richness.

Banana. *Banane* (bah-NAHN). Available at most markets and corner groceries, this fruit is not grown in France but is eaten fresh throughout the country and used in dessert making. (Travelers suffering from Montezuma's revenge should know that bananas help reverse that condition. Plus, bananas are full of potassium, so if you've lost a lot of fluids due to illness, add a banana or two to your diet for a few days.)

Basil. *Basilic* (bah-see-YEEK). Used with a liberal hand in southern France, this pungent herb goes into making *pistou* (see Menu Primer A to Z), which is mixed into soup and pasta or used as a dip for vegetables. *Pistou* is also sometimes served with roast mutton.

Bass. *Bar* (bahr) or *loup de mer* (loo duh MAIR). This fish is found on menus throughout France.

Bay leaf. *Laurier* (LOH-ree-AY). This herb is used in making a number of kinds of soups, stews, and other long-cooked dishes.

Beans. *Haricots* (AH-ree KOH). For green beans, the term *haricots verts* (ah-ree-KOH VAIR) is used. Green beans in France are very slender, darker in color than American green beans, and more intense in flavor. They are expensive and considered an elegant side dish, and once you try them, you'll know why! They're delicious, tender little morsels that are good with just about any roast meat, fish, or fowl. The term *haricot* is also used to describe dried white beans, in which case the term *haricot sec* (AH-ree-KOH SEK), or dried beans, is sometimes used. Dried white beans are often called *haricots à la bretonne* (AH-ree KOH ah lah breh-TOHN).

Beef. *Boeuf* (buhf). The French enjoy eating beef, but their consumption of it is not as high as American beef consumption. The traveler will find beef of some kind on just about every menu, at every level of dining, except perhaps at the café. *Steak frites* (see Menu Primer A to Z) are a French classic and a good menu choice if you don't know what you want to eat. Cuts of beef in France are different than in the U.S.A., so don't look for terms like "porterhouse" or "New York strip." Some of the most common cuts of beef are:

- *Bifteck* (beef-TEK). Tenderloin butt, or New York butt, cut from the larger, less tender end of the filet. The French use this term to also refer to any lean, boneless steak from the round or chuck.
- *Entrecôte* (ahn-treh-KOHT). Rib steak, or rib eye steak from the rib-roast section. It is similar to a Delmonico or club steak.
- *Faux-filet* or *contre-filet* (FOH fee-LAY or KOHN-truh fee-LAY). Loin strip steak or strip steak.
- *Romsteck* or *rumsteck* (rohm-STEK). Rump steak, cut from the end of a rump.

Beet. *Betterave* (beht-RAHV). Beets are sometimes found in composed salads at charcuteries, where they are usually served cool or at room temperature and dressed with a vinaigrette sauce.

Bill. *Addition* (ah-dee-see-OHN). This is the word to use when you ask for the check at the end of a meal.

Look the waiter in the eye and say, *"L'addition, s'il vous plaît"* (LAH-dee-SYON see-voo-play). If you think you might not be understood, make a little sign with your hand as if making a check mark on a piece of paper; I've found this tends to be a universal sign for getting the check.

Bitter. *Amer* (ah-MAIR).

Blueberry. *Myrtille* (muhr-TEE-yuh). While not exactly like American blueberries, the French version is tangier and delicious and often used in making jams.

Booked. *Complet* (kohm-PLEH). This is the word used when a restaurant is booked up and there are no tables available.

Bottle. *Bouteille* (boo-TAY-yuh).

Bowl. *Bol* (bohl).

Brains. *Cervelles* (suhr-VELL). See Menu Primer A to Z.

Brandy. *Cognac* (KOHN-yahk) and Armagnac (AHR-mahn-yahk) are the best-known brandies in France and perhaps the world; see Beverages A to Z: After-Dinner Drinks. Brandy is a spirit that is distilled from wine and aged in wood. It has a strong flavor and is quite potent. It is usually served as an after-dinner drink.

Bread. *Pain* (pan). See Menu Primer A to Z, Market Buying Tips, and Comfort Foods.

Breakfast. *Petit déjeuner* (peh-TEE DAY-jhuh-NAY). Breakfast in France is usually continental, coffee or tea and some kind of breakfast bread.

Broccoli. *Brocoli* (BROH-koh-LEE). This vegetable is sometimes served as a side dish.

Broth. *Bouillon* (boo-yohn). This may be served as a starter in some restaurants. If you're not feeling well, most sizable hotels will bring a little bouillon to your room, even if you don't see it on the room service menu.

Butter. *Beurre* (burr). Most butter in France is unsalted. Butter is a specialty of the Charente area in the Southwest, not far from Bordeaux.

Cabbage. *Chou* (shoo). This humble vegetable is eaten all over the country, especially in mountainous areas and in Alsace, where it is made into sauerkraut and served as *choucroute garnie* (see Regional/Seasonal Specialties: Alsace).

Cake. *Gâteau* (GAH-toh). French cakes can be purchased at pâtisseries (see Market Buying Tips) and enjoyed at most restaurants. French cakes tend to be quite rich and fancy, coated with butter cream, glazed with chocolate, studded with nuts, and other goodies. Unlike American cakes, which have more cake than icing, French cakes tend to be the reverse: The cake part is more of a vehicle for the very rich fillings and toppings in, over, and on top of them.

Camomile. *Camomille* (KAH-mo-MEE-yuh).

Candy. *Confiserie* (kohn-FEE-suhr-EE) or *bonbons* (bon-bon). For traditional French candies such as *pâtes des fruits* and *marrons glacées* (see Market Buying Tips), visit a specialty food store (an *épicerie*) or a chocolate shop (a *chocolaterie*).

Carrot. *Carotte* (kah-ROTT). Carrots are used in cooking (soups, stews, and broths, for instance) and served as a side dish to roasts and fish. Often they are simply parboiled, then tossed lightly in butter and perhaps sprinkled with a little chopped parsley. A popular offering in charcuteries is *carottes râpées*.

Cauliflower. *Chou-fleur* (SHOO-fluhr).

Check. *Addition* (ah-dee-see-OHN).

Cherry. *Cerise* (seh-REEZ). Found fresh in markets and cooked in desserts and jams.

Chicken. *Poulet* (poo-LAY). See Comfort Foods.

Chocolate. *Chocolat* (SHOH-koh-LAH). See Comfort Foods and Market Buying Tips: *Chocolateries*.

Cider. *Cidre* (SEE-druh). A specialty of Normandy. Be advised, French cider contains alcohol! (See Beverages A to Z: Cider.)

Clam. *Palourde* (pah-LOORD). You'll find *palourdes* on the menu in Normandy and Brittany, as well as most other parts of France.

Cocoa. *Cacao* (kah-kah-OH). This term is usually used for powdered cocoa for cooking. If you want hot chocolate, ask for *chocolat chaud* (see Comfort Foods and Beverages A to Z: Chocolate).

Coffee. *Café* (kah-FAY). It's darker and stronger in France and guaranteed to get you going in the morning. (See Beverages A to Z: Coffee.)

Cookie. *Biscuit* (bee-SKWEE). Go to any pâtisserie and you'll see an array of cookies, but not as many types as in an American bakery. You probably won't find American classics like chocolate chip and oatmeal-raisin, but you will find *sablés, macarons,* and other delights.

Crab. *Crabe* (krahb). The traveler will find good crabs in Brittany, where they are used in soup and soufflés and eaten plain. The *tourteaux* (tor-TOE) are used for crabmeat; the less meaty *araignée* (ah-rahn-yay), or spider crab, is used for soup.

Crayfish. *Écrevisses* (AY-kreh-VEES). The meat of these sweet, succulent little hard shelled critters is used for making *gratins,* sauces, and quenelles, particularly in Brittany. If you like crayfish, look for it served *à la nage,* served in fish broth with an herb-butter sauce for dipping the tails.

Cream. *Crème* (krehm). If you usually take heavy cream in your coffee, you might be out of luck at a basic café, where whole milk is usually used for making *café au lait.* The closest thing might be *crème fleurette* (krehm fluh-RETT), which is thick cream, but it is generally used in cooking, not for pouring into coffee. Whipped cream is *crème fouettée* (krehm fweh-TAY); sweetened whipped cream is *crème Chantilly* (krehm SHAN-tee-yee). *Crème fraîche* (krehm FRESH) is thick, slightly sour cream used for garnishes and in cooking.

Cucumber. *Concombre* (KOHN-KOHM-bruh).

Currant. *Cassis* (kah-SEES).

Dessert. *Dessert* (deh-SAIR). A very important word to know.

Dinner. *Dîner* (DEE-nay).

Duck. *Canard* (kah-NAHR).

Egg. *Oeuf* (uhf). See Comfort Foods.

Eggplant. *Aubergine* (oh-bair-JHEEN). A vegetable used a great deal in southern France. Ratatouille is a particularly common (and delicious) dish that the traveler will find in Provence.

Fish. *Poisson* (pwah-SOHN). As France is blessed with a long coastline, there is an abundance of fish on French menus.

Fork. *Forchette* (for-SHETT).

Free-range chicken. *Poulet fermier* (POO-lay FAIR-mee-YAY) or *poulet de grain* (POO-lay deh grehn).

French fries. *Pommes frites* (pohm FREET). See Comfort Foods.

French toast. *Pain perdu* (PAN pair-DOO). This term literally means "lost bread," which describes the way the slices of bread disappear as they soak in the milk and egg mixture. This is generally a dish prepared at home; it is not usually on restaurant menus, even at breakfast.

Fried. *Frite* (freet). If you're watching your weight, avoid foods described with the work *frite*.

Frog. *Grenouille* (grah-NOO-wee). Frogs' legs are often cooked with butter, garlic, and parsley, or they may be deep-fried, or served with lavish cream sauces. Although frogs can survive in just about any shallow pool of fresh water, wild frogs are scarce in France. Most of the frogs served in French restaurants are farm-raised, and many are imported from other countries.

Fruit. *Fruit* (fwee).

Game. *Gibier* (JHEE-bee-AY).

Garlic. *Ail* (I-yee). An ingredient used throughout France but particularly in the south. (See Regional/ Seasonal Specialties: *Provence*.)

Glass. *Verre* (vair). This word is used to describe a drinking vessel; it is also the word for mirror.

Goat. *Chèvre* (shev). See Market Buying Tips: *Fromageries*.

Goat cheese. *Fromage du chèvre* (froh-MAJH doo SHEV). See Market Buying Tips: *Fromageries*.

Goose. *Oie* (wah).

Grape. *Raisin* (ray-SAHN).

Grapefruit. *Pamplemousse* (PAHM-pluh-MOOSE).

Grilled. *Grillé* (gree-YAY). Many meats, fish, and fowl are cooked over hot coals. Look for this adjective if you're watching your fat intake, as the food described may be lighter and leaner than some other dishes on the menu. Just remember to go easy on the sauce that accompanies your grilled beef, chicken, or fish.

Ham. *Jambon* (jahm-BOHN). See Market Buying Tips: *Charcuteries*.

Herb. *Herbe* (airb).

Herb tea. *Tisane* (tee-SEHN). Most eating establishments carry some kind of herb tea; the most popular are mint *(menthe)* and camomile *(camomille)*. Tisanes are caffeine-free and usually claim to have some kind of medicinal function.

Honey. *Miel* (mee-YELL). There are very good honeys in France, and they are often used to sweeten tisanes (see above). To buy honey as a gift, go to specialty food shops or the farmers' market, where beekeepers sometimes sell their wares directly to the consumer.

Ice cream. *Glace* (glahs).

Included. *Compris* (kohm-PREE), as in "service included."

Jam. *Confiture* (KOHN-fee-TUHR). French jams are often made with less sugar than those in the States, so the flavor is truer to the fruit and not hidden by an overdose of sweetness.

Juice. *Jus* (jhoo). This word is used to describe fruit juice as well as the natural juices from cooked foods, especially meats and poultry.

Kidney. *Rognon* (ron-YON). If you like them at home, you'll love them in France.

Knife. *Couteau* (koo-TOH).

Lamb. *Agneau* (ahn-YOH).

Lamb chops. *Côte d'agneau* (kote dahn-YO).

Lavender. *Lavendre* (lah-VAHN-druh). You'll see this in Provence, not just in the countryside but at the market, where you can purchase it in dried bundles. It is sometimes used to flavor ice cream and is one of the most popular flavors of honey.

Leek. *Poireau* (pwah-RO). This humble vegetable is often used in making soups and stews.

Lemon. *Citron* (sih-TROHN).

Lemonade. *Citron pressé* (sih-TROHN preh-SAY). See Beverages A to Z.

Lettuce. *Laitue* (lah-TOO).

Lime. *Citron vert* (sih-TROHN VAIR).

Liver. *Foie* (fwah). Liver in the U.S.A. usually means calves' liver or chicken livers. In France, the word *foie* often refers to something much more elegant: *foie gras de canard* or *foie gras de oie,* the rich, unctuous liver of fattened duck or goose. *Foie gras* is usually served in small portions, on canapés, or as thin slices on salads.

Lobster. *Homard* (oh-MAHR). You'll probably find lobster on the menu in Brittany, and although it can be good, those who were raised on Maine lobster may wonder what all the fuss is about since *homard* can be stringy and tough.

Lunch. *Déjeuner* (DAY-jhuh-NAY).

Mayonnaise. *Mayonnaise* (MAH-oh-NEZ). The French enjoy it as a sauce for cooked vegetables, but you won't find it on sandwiches. Some restaurants may bring you mayonnaise for your ham and cheese if you ask, but why not do as the French do and enjoy your sandwich with a thin smear of sweet butter instead? It complements brie and jambon beautifully.

Meal. *Repas* (RE-pah).

Meat. *Viande* (vee-AHND).

Medium. *À point* (ah PWAH), as in meat.

Menu. *Carte* (kahrt).

Milk. *Lait* (lay). The French do not drink milk as a beverage, so it is not usually listed on menus as such. But, if Junior simply must have his milk, you can ask for a glass of milk *du lait* (doo lay). Be advised, however, that most milk in French restaurants is whole milk. *Café au lait,* for example, is traditionally made with whole milk, and that's what you'll be served.

Mineral water. *Eau minéral* (oh ME-nay-RAL). See Beverages A to Z: Water.

Mint. *Menthe* (mahnt).

Mushroom. *Champignon* (sham-pee-NYON). This word generally refers to firm, white button mushrooms, also known as *champignons de Paris* (sham-pee-NYON deh pah-REE) since they were at one time harvested near Paris. Wild mushrooms are usually distinguished from button mushrooms in that they are referred to by their specific name, e.g., *chanterelles* and *morilles*.

Mussels. *Moules* (mool). Mussels are served throughout France, but especially in the coastal regions, where they may be stuffed or served on huge platters with other shellfish. Big, meaty mussels from Bouzigues in Languedoc are prized throughout France.

Mustard. *Moutarde* (moo-TAHRD). Most of the mustard you'll be served in France will be the spicy, ocher-colored mustard from Dijon. (See Regional/ Seasonal Specialties: Burgundy and the Lyonnais.)

Napkin. *Serviette* (sehr-vee-YETT).

Noodle. *Nouille* (noo-EE).

Nuts. *Noix* (nwah).

Olive. *Olive* (oh-LEEV). A specialty of Provence, particularly the tiny black niçoise olive.

Omelette. *Omelette* (ahm-LETT). See Comfort Foods: Egg.

Onion. *Oignon* (on-YON). Onions and their smaller cousins, shallots, *échalotes* (ay-sha-LOTT), grow well in Bordeaux. Both are used in cooking throughout the country.

Orange. *Orange* (oh-RAHNJH).

Organic. *Biologique* (bee-oh-loh-JHEEK).

Oyster. *Huîtres* (WHEE-truh) are enjoyed throughout France, but particularly in Chablis, where they are revered and regarded by many as the perfect match for the dry, crisp white wine of the same name. Oysters are also a big part of the cuisines of Brittany and Bordeaux.

Parsley. *Persil* (pair-SEE).

Pasta. *Pâte* (paht). This word is also used to mean pastry or dough.

Pastry. *Pâtisserie* (PAH-tee-suh-REE). See Market Buying Tips: *Pâtisserie*.

Peach. *Pêche* (pesh).

Peanut. *Cacahuète* (kah-kah-WHETT).

Pear. *Poire* (pwahr).

Peas. *Pois* (pwah). This word refers to green peas. Sugar snap peas are called *mange-tout* (mahnjh-TOO), which literally means "eat it all."

Picnic. *Pique-nique* (peek-neek).

Pie. *Tarte* (tahrt). The closest equivalent to an American pie is the French *tarte*, which is usually a single-crust affair made in a tin that has a removeable bottom, so that when the tart is served, the circumference of the metal mold is removed, leaving only a circular bottom disk for support.

Pineapple. *Ananas* (ah-nah-nah).

Plate. *Assiette* (ah-see-YETT).

Plum. *Pruneau* (PROO-noh).

Pork. *Porc* (pohr).

Potable. *Potable* (poh-TAH-bluh). If you see a sign that says *eau non potable*, then do not drink the water.

Potatoes. *Pommes de terre* (POHM-deh-TAIR). See Comfort Foods: Potatoes.

Pot roast. *Pot-au-feu* (POH-toh-FUH). See Comfort Foods: Stews and stewlike dishes.

Poultry. There are several terms used for poultry. They are *poussin* (poo-SAN), a very young, small chicken; *poulet* (poo-LAY), a tender young spring chicken; and *poularde* (poo-LAHRD), a roasting chicken. (See also Comfort Foods: Chicken.)

Prawn. *Langoustine* (LAHN-goo-STEEN).

Price. *Prix* (pree).

Rabbit. *Lapin* (lah-PAN).(See Menu Primer A to Z.

Raisin. *Raisin sec* (ray-SAN SEK). The term literally means "dry grape."

Rare. *Bleu* (bluh) or *saignant* (sayn-YAHN), as in meat.

Raspberry. *Framboise* (fram-BWAHZ).

Receipt. *Reçu* (reh-SOO) is for a written receipt; *ticket* (tee-KAY) is for a cash register receipt.

Reservation. *Reservation* (REH-zehr-VAH-see-OHN).

Rice. *Riz* (ree).

Salmon. *Saumon* (soh-MAHN).

Salt. *Sel* (sell).

Sauce. *Sauce* (soss).

Scallops. *Coquilles Saint-Jacques* (kon-KEEL sahn-JHAHK).

Scampi. *Crevettes* (kreh-VETT).

Service. *Service* (sehr-VEES).

Service included. *Service inclus* (sehr-VEE-sahn-KLOO).

Shellfish. *Crustacés* (kru-sta-SAY). This term includes scampi, lobster, crayfish, and crab.

Shrimp. *Crevettes* (kreh-VEHT). (See Scampi above.)

Smoked. *Fumé* (FOO-may).

Snail. *Escargots* (ESS-kar-GOH). A specialty of Bordeaux but served throughout France. The best snails, say connoisseurs, are the large, beige *escargot de Bourgogne,* and the best time to gather them is in the late fall when they are hibernating since they tend to be fatter then. *Petits gris* (PEH-tee gree) snails are smaller than Burgundy snails but are more common.

Sole. *Sole* (sohl).

Soup. *Soupe* (soop). See Comfort Foods.

Spinach. *Épinard* (AY-pee-NAHRD). Even in France, spinach is spinach, and your kids won't eat it.

Spoon. *Cuillère* (koo-YAIR).

Squid. *Calmar* (kal-MAHR).

Steak. *Bifteck* (BEEF-tek).

Strawberry. *Fraise* (frehz).

Sugar. *Sucre* (SOO-kruh). Most of the sugar served with coffee and tea in France will be in lump form. Watch the locals as they stir, stir, stir that tiny cup of espresso to melt the sugar cubes.

Sweetbreads *(of young calves). Ris de veau* (REE-deh VOH).

Sweet pepper. *Poivron* (pwah-ROHN). See Regional/ Seasonal Specialties: The Pays Basque, Gascony, and the Pyrénées.

Tablecloth. *Nappe* (nahp).

Tea. *Thé* (tay).
Tip. *Service* (sehr-VEES).
Toast. *Pain grillé* (pan gree-YAY).
Tomato. *Tomate* (toh-MAHT).
Tongue. *Langue* (lahng).
Tripe. *Tripe* (treep). A specialty of Caen, in Normandy.
Tuna. *Thon* (tohn).
Turkey. *Dinde* (dahnd).
Turnip. *Navet* (nah-VAY).
Vanilla. *Vanille* (vah-NEE-yuh).
Veal. *Veau* (voh).
Vegetables. *Légumes* (lay-GOOM).
Vinegar. *Vinaigre* (val-NAI-gruh).
Waiter. *Serveur* (sehr-VUHR).
Waitress. *Serveuse* (sehr-VUHZ).
Walnut. *Noix* (nwah).
Wheat. *Blé* (blay).
Wine. *Vin* (van). See Beverages A to Z: Wine.
Wine list. *Carte des vins* (kahrt des van).
Wine steward. *Sommelier* (soh-mahl-YAY) or *Sommelière* (if female). (See Beverages A to Z: Wine.)
Yogurt. *Yaourt* (YA-uhr) or *yoghourt* (YO-guhr).
Zucchini. *Courgette* (koor-JHETT).